# CHILE

# CHILE

## The Great Transformation

*Javier Martínez* and *Alvaro Díaz*

THE BROOKINGS INSTITUTION *Washington, D.C.*
and
THE UNITED NATIONS RESEARCH INSTITUTE FOR
SOCIAL DEVELOPMENT *Geneva*

*Copyright © 1996 by*
THE UNITED NATIONS RESEARCH INSTITUTE FOR SOCIAL DEVELOPMENT (UNRISD)
*Palais des Nations CH-1211 Geneva 10, Switzerland*

*Library of Congress Cataloging-in-Publication data:*

Martínez Bengoa, Javier.
    Chile, the great transformation / Javier Martínez, Alvaro Díaz.
       p.   cm.
    ISBN 0-8157-5478-7 (cl : alk. paper). — ISBN 0-8157-5477-9 (pa :
alk. paper)
    1. Chile—Economic conditions—1973–1988.   2. Chile—Economic
conditions—1988–    3. Chile—Politics and government—1973–
I. Díaz Pérez, Alvaro H.    II. Title.
HC192.M34   1996
338.983—dc20

95-52628
CIP

9 8 7 6 5 4 3 2 1

The paper used in this publication meets the minimum
requirements of the American National Standard for
Information Sciences—Permanence of Paper for Printed
Library Materials, ANSI Z39.48—1984

Set in Garamond Book

Composition by Harlowe Typography Inc.,
Cottage City, Maryland

Printed by R. R. Donnelley & Sons Co.
Harrisonburg, Virginia

*To the memory of*
*Fernando Fajnzylber*

# Preface

The international development community is often too quick to generalize. When one country or region adapts relatively successfully to economic crisis, for example, others are immediately urged to emulate its policies, without necessarily giving sufficient attention to the specific nature of local society or to the historical foundations of local institutions.

This could certainly be said of the Chilean "success story" in the field of structural adjustment and market reform. Governments from Russia and Mexico to Bangladesh have frequently been urged to follow the Chilean example. But since the resource endowments, cultures, demographics, and economic and political systems of these countries may differ markedly from those of Chile, there is no reason to expect that transplanted policies will produce a standard result.

Chile is a small, highly urbanized country with a relatively strong tradition of parliamentary democracy and judicial independence, as well as a system of public services well known in Latin America for its efficiency and lack of corruption. Its population density and birth rate are low, and (when compared with many other societies) its culture is homogeneous. Nevertheless, like many other Latin American countries, Chile long suffered the economic difficulties associated with dependence upon the export of primary products and the unresolved tensions of industrialization within small, protected markets. By the early 1970s, the country was involved in a highly contentious transition to socialism, under a democratically elected government, which ended in one of the bloodiest military coups of recent Latin American history. Free-market restructuring was subsequently carried out within a strongly authoritarian context by a government that could seriously affect the interests of allies, as well as opponents, with impunity.

In *Chile: The Great Transformation*, two distinguished Chilean social scientists attempt to explain their country's experience with neoliberal reform to an international audience. This is not a technical economic study, but a political and institutional analysis of a singular process of socioeconomic transformation. It challenges the reader to understand longer-term processes, as well as the immediate tactical measures, that conditioned the reform effort and determined its outcome. And it describes Chilean society today, as the country attempts to consolidate a return to democracy and to attack the extreme inequality, job insecurity, and external vulnerability that are the legacy of the past twenty years.

The study was commissioned by the United Nations Research Institute for Social Development (UNRISD) as part of its comparative research program on *Crisis, Adjustment and Social Change in Latin America*, directed by Cynthia Hewitt de Alcántara. The collaborating Chilean institution was SUR Profesionales Consultores, Ltd., of Santiago. UNRISD would like to thank Benjamin Richards for his able translation of the original Spanish manuscript and Irene Ruíz de Budavari and Anita Tombez for their excellent secretarial support. Nancy Davidson, of the Brookings Institution, served as a careful and committed editor. Funding for the project was provided through a generous grant from the Government of the Netherlands.

Dharam Ghai
Director, UNRISD

# Contents

## Tables

## Figures

# Introduction

Situated in the extreme south of the American continent, isolated by the massive Andean mountain range and the vast Pacific Ocean, and endowed with a geography almost implausible in its length and narrowness, Chile is considered by many analysts to be one of the great modern laboratories of political experimentation. As if Chileans need to remind the outside world of their presence, the country has overcome its physical isolation to embrace great international currents of thought. More than once, especially during this century, Chile's position at the center of political events has had far-reaching consequences.

Recent Chilean history has been no exception: two substantial achievements have brought Chile into the world spotlight. First, more than a decade of sustained economic growth, averaging 7 percent annually, has made Chile the most dynamic economy in Latin America. Second, after a period of acute political conflict, culminating in one of the most infamous dictatorships in history, Chile has reestablished its democratic system through a transition exemplary for its efficient and peaceful nature. The "Chilean model" has become a commonly heard phrase, although it is full of contradictions. It is used by proponents of "structural adjustment," by those calling for dictatorship, by those promoting grand democratic transformations, and by those seeking to reduce social inequalities, as well as those who see in such inequalities an invaluable source of social dynamism.

This diversity of opinion testifies to the complexity of the great transformation that has taken place in Chile, a process that consequently requires careful and detailed analysis. The underlying thesis of this book is that Chile has experienced an authentic capitalist revolution and not just a process of structural adjustment. Like all revolutions, it is a process with many contradictions, and there is no room for sim-

1

plistic interpretations. It is the product of unique historical circumstances and cannot be reduced to yet another case within the so-called general laws of history. Like all revolutions worthy of the name, however, this great Chilean transformation is full of global implications.

The Chilean experience has been the source of intense ideological debates. These have often been excessively partisan and as a consequence have given rise to distorted interpretations that nevertheless enjoy considerable currency. This book purports to show that many of the ideological explanations currently associated with the Chilean experience, both within the country and abroad, have little historical foundation. This will be shown in some detail in the chapters that follow, but it is necessary to draw attention to four ideas that, in spite of the political lessons often drawn from them and their widespread acceptance, are completely false.

## First Fallacy

The first fallacy is that the success of the economic transformation in Chile was due to the dictatorial nature of the Pinochet regime, which was responsible for carrying it out.

The right-wing version of this argument attempts to demonstrate that dictatorships are necessary in other countries. The left-wing version, using the same false logic, attempts to argue against economic liberalization in other countries.

Certainly the most fundamental stage of economic transformation in Chile took place *during* the military dictatorship headed by General Augusto Pinochet and was promoted and imposed by the economic team chosen and supported by the military. Yet the military dictatorship emerged in Chile as a reaction to the unmanageable situation brought on by the social struggles that accompanied the reforms of the government of Salvador Allende. The junta's claim to legitimacy was based on the restoration of political order, not economic transformation. Only later, as a result of the radical nature of the military intervention—and following the historical pattern of the few military interventions in Chilean politics—did the necessity emerge for an equally radical economic program.

It is necessary to go beyond the strictly episodic aspects of the Chilean experience, however, and ask to what extent the dictatorial nature of the political regime was essential to the transformation of the economy, and, furthermore, to the success of this transformation. This study argues that it was not so much the regime's use of force, but rather its autonomy from the immediate interests of the social groups that had brought it to power, that permitted the Pinochet government to carry out a complete restructuring of Chilean capitalism. The two are not equivalent: not all dictatorships have such relative autonomy, especially in terms of executive power, nor do other types of regimes necessarily lack it.

It is sufficient to point out that Latin American history has been plagued with military dictatorships—many of a personalized nature, but others as institutionalized as that of Pinochet, if not more so—that have done nothing to create a new type of economic order. Equally, the recent experiences of free-market transformations in countries such as Mexico, Bolivia, and even Argentina show that autonomy is more closely linked to the magnitude of the economic crisis than to the nature of the political regime.

To this must be added a factor that is rarely mentioned and that constitutes a reverse argument. One of the biggest threats to the success of the Chilean economic transformation, shown clearly by an examination of the economic policy implemented between 1978 and 1983, was the *rigidity* of the decisionmaking process, which arose out of the dictatorial nature of the regime at the time.

## Second Fallacy

The second fallacy is that the return to democracy in Chile was the result of the success of the economic transformation. This fallacy is closely associated with the kind of crude materialism of both the free-market ideology, currently in vogue, and the Marxist concept of "bourgeois democracy." If democracy has ever emerged out of a capitalist revolution, this was certainly not the case in Chile.

Democracy has a long tradition in Chile, and the persistent symbolic importance of this tradition was the biggest obstacle to Pinochet's attempts to remain in power. Even more important, it is absolutely clear that the recovery of democracy in Chile arose from a profound mass rebellion against the Pinochet dictatorship. This was ultimately to express itself through the old party elites, who triumphed through the use of the very institutional mechanisms designed by the authoritarian regime to perpetuate its power.

For this reason, students of the relationship between politics and economics must ask themselves questions that turn crude materialism on its head: why did the consolidation of democracy in Chile require the defeat of the political regime that had been fundamental in securing the future of capitalism there? The relative autonomy of the political system, and the way this produced the conditions that would permit the return to democracy, are issues that require careful attention and find particular resonance in the Chilean case.

## Third Fallacy

The third fallacy is that the process of nationalization and state intervention, during the period before the implementation of the free-market model, represented an important obstacle to the realization and success of this model.

This fallacy is the Chilean version of the well-known Polish joke: "What is socialism?" asks the first Pole. "The longest route to capitalism," answers the second. Nevertheless, at least in this case, the joke has no historical grounding, not only because of the brevity of the socialist experience and the lengthiness of the dictatorship that led to the capitalist revolution, but also because the dictatorship was able to build its success on the effects of the socialist experience.

Upon taking power in Chile, the military dictatorship found that many of the social relations formerly cementing the Chilean economic structure were in a state of flux. Large landowners had been destroyed by the massive expropriations associated with agrarian reform, the entire banking system had been nationalized, a large part of industry was owned or controlled by the state, and the copper industry—which produced the basic Chilean export—had been nationalized. The modernizing, and not simply reactionary, nature of the Pinochet dictatorship was most clearly demonstrated in the way it managed to redirect rather than reverse these earlier transformations.

This issue is examined in greater detail in the following chapters. It is sufficient here to consider the transformation of agriculture—the basis for the new export model—as an example. During the Pinochet period, only a third of the land expropriated under the agrarian reform programs of previous governments was returned to its original owners. Moreover, this was not the land that had previously formed part of the *latifundio* system. The rest was distributed in smallholdings to peasants—as provided for by the agrarian reform program—but without the technical assistance and credit the program had envisaged. The result was the massive sale of this land, appropriate for capitalist development, and the establishment of a land market. This was particularly important because for centuries inheritance of excessively large holdings had proved a major obstacle to dynamism and productivity in the countryside.

The social base that supported Pinochet would certainly not have allowed a massive expropriation program such as that which had been carried out by earlier governments against a powerful landowning oligarchy. But the weakness of this class after the reform, and the relative autonomy this gave to the regime, encouraged the development of capitalist relations in the countryside. This was done without losing the support of the oligarchy, who benefited from the bonds paid by the exchequer. Furthermore, these payments swelled the funds that could be utilized by a new and hungry financial sector.

Similar processes can be observed in industry, banking, and mining. Far from representing obstacles, the previous socializing reforms provided opportunities for the restructuring of an underdeveloped capitalism, which at the time was burdened not only by a "crisis of the welfare state," as the free-market ideologues claimed, but also by the continued existence of feudal and paternalistic relations. The reforms of the Pinochet period were based on privatizing state assets, but *not* upon a restoration of the traditional social order in Chile, because the social forces that could have supported such a restoration were too weak. This was a fundamental element in the success of the transformation carried out between 1973 and 1990.

## Fourth Fallacy

The fourth fallacy is that the Chilean experience represents yet another example of the development of capitalism through the means of a civic rebellion against the state, limiting its sphere of action and thus extending individual liberties.

To put it absolutely bluntly, there is no similarity between Pinochet and Cromwell, apart from the fact that they both closed their respective parliaments. The Chilean transformation can be described as a capitalist revolution but not a bourgeois revolution.

It is at exactly this point that the "mystery" of the relationship between capitalism and democracy is to be found in the Chilean case. In contrast to the Anglo-Saxon model, civil society in Chile is the child of the state, brought into existence prematurely by the necessities of the long and ferocious Araucanian war waged against an indigenous resistance that lasted for the not inconsiderable period of 300 years. A well-known historian characterizes the birth of Chilean society in the following way: "The fundamental nature of Chile under the Spanish empire is that of a battle frontier, a land of war."[1]

To these origins, which left a deep mark on the conquest and colonial periods, can be added the first century of the independent republic that emerged in 1810: the Araucanian war, which lasted until 1883, the nineteenth-century wars of independence that continued in the south, the campaign for liberation from Peru, the war against the Peruvian-Bolivian confederation between 1836 and 1839, the naval war against Spain (1864–66), the war of the Pacific (1879–83), and the civil war of 1891. For this reason, according to the same historian, "the Chilean nation was formed by a state which preceded it. This was a process similar to that of Argentina, but different from that of Mexico and Peru, where great indigenous cultures preceded the Viceroys and the Republics."

The state in Chile not only preceded civil society, but, more important, it was also its creator, the artist who shaped every one of its features. The maintenance of an army constantly at war implied significant expense for both the Spanish crown and the Republican government that followed it during the nineteenth century. But the private economy was also able to develop in close association with the success of the military campaigns. Even more important, the expansion of the state in Chile from the beginning of the twentieth century not only imposed a growing burden on the domestic private sector but also assisted its development. The two great sources of state revenues were nitrates and copper. The negotiations with foreign investors allowed the state a certain autonomy in terms of development, which avoided conflict with domestic capitalists. Income from copper, administered by a middle-class bureaucracy that expanded greatly once the cycle of wars ended (and was for a long time more modernizing and dynamic than the private sector), was later used to subsidize industrialization and create a national bourgeoisie. This bourgeoisie was the child of the modern state, not its parent.

This study argues that the great economic transformation that has taken place in Chile is in line with this general historical process. It was the development of a state elite, rather than the existence of previously constituted social classes, that permitted the capitalist revolution of recent decades. And if this was a revolution, rather than a new era of reforms, it was precisely because it finally managed to change the historical relationship between state and society that had characterized the country since its birth.

How lasting will the effects of this transformation be? The stage is set for the appearance of new actors. The economic transformation carried out from the state by a technocratic elite has paved the way for a new and innovative business class. Meanwhile, the political transformation caused by mass rebellion has permitted the emergence of a new civilian political class, distanced from the old ideological confrontations and clearly oriented toward the construction of a new consensus. The key to the Chilean transition lies in the possibility of forming a working alliance among these new actors. But this requires the emancipation of all groups from the specific circumstances that gave birth to them— and this is a process that is only just beginning.

# 1

## Politics: From Dictatorship to Democracy

The final recourse of the state is force, and therefore the fundamental instinct of politics is fear. Successive theorists from Macchiavelli, Hobbes, and Marx to Max Weber have drawn attention to this fact: the efficiency of the state is derived from its brutal nature, although to achieve legitimacy it must also present its human, rational, or beatific face.

For a time in the twentieth century it appeared that Chileans had been spared this basic principle of politics. A prolonged period of stability of democratic-republican institutions, exceptional in the Latin American context, generated the illusion that any type of change was possible in the country through legal, peaceful, and rational means. The great slogans of social transformation during the 1960s were evidence of this: the "revolution in liberty" and the "peaceful road to socialism."

This perception was not completely unfounded, although it might be considered a little naive. Reforms far less radical than those that took place in Chile between 1964 and 1970 provoked revolutions and serious conflicts in other countries. And, at least from the 1930s on, general respect for the law in Chile was strong enough to weaken significantly the power of those who wished to flout it.

The explanation for this relative institutional stability is simple. From 1925 on, the party system and the permanent apparatus of the state were ruled by a modernizing middle class, which established a solid center of gravity around which power struggles and decisions circulated. By 1973, however, this center had begun to lose all of its capacity to perform such a role.

## Instability

The collapse of the political center is closely related to developments within the Chilean party system at the beginning of the 1950s. A basically pragmatic and coalition-seeking group (the Radical party) was replaced by a reforming current with a strong ideological or doctrinaire content (Christian Democracy) whose leadership habitually rejected coalition and affirmed the idea of an independent political force.

This displacement of the Radical party from the center was the result of a recomposition of the party system in response to the eruption of a national-populist alternative, headed by General Carlos Ibáñez del Campo, in 1952. Since the end of the first quarter of the century, the group of traditional political parties (composed of conservatives and other social-Christian, liberal, radical, socialist, and communist forces) had normally managed to represent more than 80 percent of the electorate. The agreements formed within the party establishment—whose axis was the social democrat–leaning Radical party—meant that it had acquired a strong national legitimacy. In 1952, however, General Ibáñez, supported by a diverse extraparty base that expressed a bitter rejection of political negotiation, and finding wide sympathy among the politically marginalized masses, achieved an almost outright majority in his candidacy for the presidency of the republic. This was evidence of a crisis of representation in the formal party system and the onset of a rupture between the permanent bodies of the Chilean state and its representative bodies.[1]

In contrast to other Latin American experiences, however, national-populism as manifested in the *ibañista* phenomenon did not succeed in consolidating itself as a political movement that transcended its experience in government. Reluctance to use the state to organize the masses originally giving it support—in the style of typical populist experiences—contributed to this outcome. In addition, within the context of a new outbreak of inflation, Ibáñez was forced to seek the support of a rival section of the party system (the liberal-conservative right) in order to strengthen his stabilization policies.

In spite of the fact that the *ibañista* period did not lead to full-fledged incorporation of the marginal sectors, the masses became, from that time on, a fundamental factor in Chilean politics. Furthermore, the recomposition of the party system could no longer ignore them. The coalition arrangements that took place on a purely party level, and allowed for the representation of the already integrated or "historic" segments of the population, lost their relative importance in the face of the competition to represent new sectors, recently incorporated into political citizenship. Political parties consequently turned their attention to women, marginal urban sectors, peasants, and youth.

The failure of *ibañismo*, and the difficult adaptation of the party machinery in the face of the new importance of the masses, favored the appearance of *caudillismo* and the convergence of the parties behind charismatic national leaders. Above all, the realignment produced a shift in the political center, already mentioned, in favor of the Christian Democrats, a party whose doctrinaire stance and unwillingness to enter coalitions allowed the representation of demands against the official political establishment. In 1949 the Christian Democrat party (then known as Falange Nacional) represented only 3.9 percent of the electorate compared with 21.7 percent for the Radical party, while twenty years later the Christian Democrats' share had grown to 31.1 percent compared with 13.6 percent for the Radical party.

During the administration of Eduardo Frei (1964–70), the Christian Democrats attempted to incorporate their supporters among the marginal masses. This was done through a wide range of reforms that consolidated the party's electoral position but increased its political isolation. While the left grew systematically through its demands for a radicalization of the reforms, the right regrouped through a policy of aggressive opposition.[2] In contrast to the situation at the beginning of the 1950s, there were now no possibilities for an expansion of the frontiers of the party system. The masses who had previously been marginalized no longer lacked leadership. On the contrary, they were fully mobilized within the context of the party struggle. This had three important consequences. First, the Christian Democrat party—faced with an important internal division involving its left wing—became incapable of forming a coalition with either of the two poles of the electoral spectrum (which permitted the victory in 1970 of Salvador Allende and Popular Unity with a little over a third of the vote). Second, the party system found itself facing a situation of extreme rigidity that prevented it from producing consensual solutions when confronted by crisis situations (as can be seen toward the end of the Frei government, when it was faced with an aborted military uprising). Third, the right had the best chance of leading the extra-institutional mobilization against the reform policies of Popular Unity, the basis for which had been laid during the Christian Democratic government.

In the field of civil politics, the collapse of a possible agreement with the center was already evident as the end of the Popular Unity government approached in 1973. Although the Christian Democrats continued to be the biggest single party in terms of electoral strength—a fact that was made clear in the parliamentary elections of March 1973—the potential for representative politics to provide a solution to the impasse had been drastically reduced in the face of the daily eruption of mass confrontation. Parliament had simply become a sounding board for a political struggle that was taking place in the streets, factories, and educational institutions. Under these circumstances, the forms of mobilization in opposition to Allende's government were imposed by the Christian Democrats' allies on the extreme right.[3]

After the fact, some analysts, particularly many of the participants in the military rebellion of 1973, have tried to present the rebellion against Allende as having been motivated by a decision to give the country new political institutions. This is very far from the truth. In contrast to what might be said about the economy, the military junta seizing power in 1973 did not arrive bearing any new model of political institutionality for the country. The military took power not in favor of a project of social recomposition but rather against what the Popular Unity government was trying to bring about. The military coup was, in the strictest sense of the word, reactionary. Moreover, it is probable that within the armed forces, as was clearly the case among civilians, many officers saw their action as a drastic measure directed toward the restoration of a social, economic, and political order broken by the turbulent years of Popular Unity, and not as an attempt to replace it with a new type of order.

If the radicalization of the struggle of the masses during the Popular Unity period ( 1970–73 ) left the center with no capacity for taking the political initiative in the civil sphere, then the incorporation of the commanders-in-chief of the armed forces into the ministerial cabinet in the last months of the Allende government, as well as the extreme violence of the 1973 coup, had a similar effect inside the armed forces. The incorporation of the military chiefs into Allende's cabinet led, in effect, to a rapid deterioration of his authority before the body of senior officers. At the same time, the first weeks of massive detentions, firing squads, and summary executions that followed the military coup, and, above all, the bombardment of the presidential palace, leading to the death of the constitutional president, ruled out any possibility of a speedy return to institutional normality. Instead, it necessitated the search for a new institutional model that would justify a long stay in power for the armed forces.[4]

The disproportionate violence of the coup burned the bridges with the previous political system and gave rise to the need for a new institutional order. For this reason, a number of contradictory signals were given immediately after the coup as to the nature of the political model that the military was ultimately seeking to impose. Clearly indicative of this were the declarations of two members of the junta in the two weeks following the coup. On September 17, 1973, in an interview with the *New York Times*, General Pinochet stated that there would be elections "when the country returns to normality and the unity of all Chileans, and of Chile as a Nation and as a State, is sufficiently strong to guarantee a return to its traditional and exemplary democratic republican path." Nevertheless, another member of the junta, Air Force General Gustavo Leigh, announced four days later that a new constitution was being prepared that would reflect the "entire nation," giving representation to the armed forces, the police, the professional organizations, women, and youth. This constitution would not, however, be subject to a popular vote for its ratification.

These contradictory models—republican and corporatist—had common reactionary elements. The first was the need to "struggle to the death against Marxism"—understanding this to be the parties that had constituted the Allende government, as well as its intellectual and trade union supporters. The second was the decision not to negotiate or give ground to the political center, represented by the Christian Democrats. The third was the decision to stay in power without calling elections, given that those two political blocs together represented three-quarters of the electorate. Finally, but no less important, the political leadership of the military came together in a common disdain for the civilian political class, which was translated into a desire to give the armed forces a permanent political role in the life of the nation. It is this entirely reactive character of the military consensus, to which a founding spirit was completely foreign, that explains the dominant mood between 1973 and 1983.

## The Terror

The leadership contest within the new regime was marked by attempts to give the greatest demonstration of commitment to this reactionary consensus, and this became a competition as to who could best represent authoritarian extremism. For Chilean society, the consequence of this was years of terror.

On September 13, 1973, the National Congress was officially dissolved, which led to the final disappearance of the hopes of the political center. The next day, the political parties forming the Popular Unity coalition that had supported ex-President Allende were declared illegal. On September 26, the Central Union of Workers (CUT) was also outlawed "for having assumed the character of a political organization." That same day, all the jailed members of the armed ultraright movement Fatherland and Freedom (Patria y Libertad) were released. On September 27, the junta declared all political parties "in recess," including those that had headed the struggle against the Allende regime. (Months later, in January 1974, the junta announced that "non-Marxist" parties could carry out administrative activities, with any political action still prohibited. This prohibition included distributing propaganda, holding meetings, or participating in organizations such as unions or student federations.) The parties were ordered to submit to the Ministry of the Interior a list of all their militants before October 11, 1973. The electoral register was cancelled in November 1973 and destroyed by order of the junta in July 1974. From the day of the coup, the country was declared in "a state of internal war" and the states of siege and emergency were renewed at one time or another for over a decade. In terms of the judiciary, although the new regime had already been recognized by the Supreme Court on September 13, around the middle of November of that year the junta announced that the decisions of military tribunals could not be the subject of appeals to the Supreme Court.

Even now, the estimates of the number of dead, disappeared, injured, prisoners, and exiles in the first months of the coup and under martial law remain the subject of conjecture. In terms of the number killed, a report from the U.S. State Department cited by Senator Edward Kennedy on February 3, 1974, confirmed that there were "several thousand," although the specific estimates were classified as confidential. A month after the coup, on October 10, 1973, the junta stated officially that 513 civilians and 37 soldiers had been killed since September 11. Since the military took power, 5,400 people had been detained. "Only 94 summary executions" were recognized as having been carried out by the beginning of November. Amnesty International, on January 20, 1974, stated in a letter to General Augusto Pinochet that a commission of the organization had been able to prove "widespread torture" of political detainees. The junta, nevertheless, did not accept this version of events and systematically denied any type of human rights violations in Chile.

In terms of exiles, the official statistics provided by the junta in the middle of February 1974 indicated that between September 11, 1973, and February 12, 1974, the exit of 7,317 people classified as refugees had been permitted. Of these, 4,000 had sought asylum in embassies, where 243 still remained as refugees. The figures given by opponents of the junta were far greater. In November 1973, for example, ex-Senator Carlos Altamirano (on whose head the new government had placed an official price) declared in a press conference in Havana after his clandestine flight from the country that "more than 15,000 people had been killed," that there were "more than 30,000 political detainees," that "tens of thousands" had been tortured, more than a million people had lost their jobs, and 25,000 students had been expelled from the universities.

It is difficult to arrive at an exact quantitative estimate of the violation of human rights during the first months of military government, not only because the respective information was always kept strictly secret, but because the repression was carried out in those days by a variety of organizations with little reciprocal coordination. What is certain, however, is that terror had taken its grip on Chilean politics, and the very uncertainty of information was part of this process.

It was not, of course, to be an isolated situation in Latin America. Following the military coup in Chile, seven of the eleven independent South American countries were under military governments (Bolivia, Brazil, Ecuador, Paraguay, Peru, and Uruguay, joined by Argentina in 1976). This means that 68 percent of the population and 74 percent of the territory of South America were, at this time, governed by this type of regime.

The terror continued to increase in the years following the coup. To the hundreds of denunciations of arbitrary detention, torture, and disappearance of prisoners were added murky cases of international state terrorism. The most prominent cases were the assassination in Buenos Aires of the previous commander-in-chief of the army and former minister of the interior and defense, General Carlos Prats, and his wife on September 30, 1974; the attempt on the life of the former vice president of the republic and former minister of the interior during the Christian Democrat government of Eduardo Frei, Bernardo Leighton, and his wife in Rome on October 6, 1975; and the assassination of Orlando Letelier, former vice president of the republic and former foreign minister, interior minister, and defense minister, together with his secretary, Ronnie Moffit, in Washington, D.C., on September 21, 1976.

The concentration of power in the hands of the chief of the military junta also continued to increase. In February 1974 the retirement of two army generals, Orlando Urbina Herrera and Manuel Torres de la Cruz, who were immediately beneath the commander-in-chief in the line of succession, was announced. Following these retirements, in March 1975 the defense minister and one of the coup leaders in the army, General Oscar Bonilla, were killed when the helicopter in which they were traveling crashed.

On June 26, 1974, in a first move toward the institutionalization of military rule, the commander-in-chief of the army (General Augusto Pinochet) was designated "supreme head of the nation" by decree of the military junta. The junta officially took over legislative and executive powers, and it was established that General Pinochet would continue to head the junta in charge of the administration and government of the country. In the event of his death or resignation he would be replaced by the most senior remaining member of the collegiate body. Not long afterward, by virtue of a secret decree, a powerful political police organization (the National Intelligence Directive, or DINA) was created, which was responsible only to the head of state. On December 17, 1974, General Pinochet was officially designated "president of the republic" through a decree signed by himself and the three other members of the junta. This established that from then on Pinochet would retain executive power while the military junta would assume legislative power.

The concentration of power in the hands of General Pinochet would be marked by two other especially important milestones, both linked to plebiscitary forms of legitimization. These broke with the prevailing logic of taking decisions through an agreement between the chiefs of the different branches of the armed forces.

The first instance in which citizens were called to express themselves took place at the beginning of 1978. This had its origin, according to the official explanation, in a resolution of the General Assembly of the United Nations (Resolution 32/118), which reiterated the "profound indignation" of the General Assembly at the fact that "the Chilean people continues to be the object of constant and flagrant violations of human rights and fundamental liberties, the absence of adequate constitutional and judicial safeguards to their rights and liberties, attempts against the liberty and integrity of the individual, in particular through methods of systematic intimidation, including torture, disappearance of people for political reasons, arbitrary arrests, detentions, exile and deprivation of Chilean nationality."

The response of the head of the military government was to call a "national consultation" on December 21, 1977. All Chileans over the age of 18 were called upon to vote, within two weeks, for or against the following affirmation: "In the face of international aggression against our country, I support President Pinochet in his defense of the dignity of Chile and reaffirm the legitimacy of the government of the republic as sovereign leader in the process of institutionalization of the country."

The calling of this singular "consultation" provoked opposition from within the military junta itself, two of whose members sent letters to this effect to General Pinochet. Of these, the contents of the letter signed by Commander-in-Chief of the Air Force Gustavo Leigh were made public. Leigh protested, in the name of his institution, that the "honor and prestige" of the armed forces would be compromised by having to supervise a plebiscite that "by its very nature will give rise to suspicion and misinterpretation." He added that the calling of the plebiscite was contrary to the statutes established by the military government itself and that it had been communicated to the other members of the military junta only one day before its public announcement, without specifying its actual content. The comptroller general of the republic resigned his post on December 28 after having rejected the procedure for the calling of the consultation. He was replaced the same day by a minister of the military government.

The referendum took place on January 4, 1978, and, according to official results, 75 percent of Chileans voted in favor of the only alternative given. General Gustavo Leigh was sacked from his post as commander-in-chief of the air force, together with twelve generals who followed him in the line of succession. The leadership of Pinochet within the army, and the predominance of that institution over the other bodies of the armed forces, was absolutely clear. Above all, a form of Caesarist legitimization of presidential power had been tested that would soon come to be used as the principal mechanism for political institutionalization.

The most audacious step in this direction would take place two years later. On August 10, 1979, General Pinochet announced a new plebiscite, this time with the purpose of approving a political constitution to replace the old one of 1925. The definitive text of this new document corresponded broadly to the recommendations put forward by the Council of State, an advisory organ to the military junta headed by the constitutional ex-president (1958–64), Jorge Alessandri Rodríguez. Nevertheless, the text also included a "transitory article" that set out an itinerary for "slow and gradual transition to full democracy." General Pinochet would rule for eight more years, at the end of which the military junta would propose a single candidate for the presidency for another eight years (which could be General Pinochet again). This would then be voted on by the people in a new plebiscite designed to approve or reject the proposal. During the eight-year transition period, the permanent aspects of the new constitution would not be put into force completely, except for those that did not contradict the transitory articles.

As with the earlier plebiscite, the vote took place a few weeks after being called, without a public electoral register and with continued prohibition of expression on the part of political parties. According to official figures, 67 percent voted for the constitution and 30.2 percent against. Spoiled votes amounted to 2.8 percent (blank ballot papers were counted as approval). This was the decisive step in the consolidation of the power of the commander-in-chief of the army and his autonomy from the other heads of the armed forces.

The absence of counterweights within the new power structure was exacerbated by the extreme weakness of social movements, owing to fierce repression and the persistence of political divisions from the immediate past, and—no less important—the economic situation and very high rates of unemployment. In effect, apart from some skirmishes with unions and students—which were important only to the extent that they increased friction within the power bloc—the junta did not encounter significant social resistance to its political dominance. What did stand in the way of military power, at least during the first decade of the dictatorship, was not really a political alternative, but rather a "zone of refuge" in the form of the Catholic Church.

The institutional commitment of the Catholic Church to the defense of human rights began toward the end of 1973 when, together with other churches, it joined the Committee of Cooperation for Peace in Chile. The committee was to give help to political detainees and assist their relatives in the search for information. This commitment was soon deepened with the creation of the Vicariate of Solidarity. Dependent on the archbishop of Santiago, this became the most active agent of protection, denunciation, and promotion in the field of human rights, once state political repression had become institutionally centralized (first in the DINA and then in the National Intelligence Center, or CNI).

In the absence of any institutionally recognized forms of social participation, the political system, in the first ten years of the military regime, took on the characteristics of the old days of the conquest. Political parties were declared illegal or forbidden from organizing, and social organizations independent of the regime were persecuted. In this situation there were only two relevant actors: a "captain-general" in charge of political power, sustained by force of arms and emergency legislation giving him unlimited powers,[5] and the Catholic Church as an open refuge for persecuted civilians. This clearly indicates that, far from advancing toward a new form of legal institutionalization, the state of exception was becoming a permanent feature.

## The Uprising

As the beginning of the democratization process, 1983 and 1984 marked an important turning point in the Chilean political situation. After ten years of fierce military government, during which the only important opposition against persistent human rights violations was the defensive shield of the Catholic Church, a period of civil rebellion began. This was most clearly seen in the "days of protest" against the dictatorship.

The catalyst for this unexpected movement was a call, made in April 1983 by the powerful Confederation of Copper Workers (CTC), for a national strike against the policies of the regime. This was later modified to a call for all sectors to protest, actively and peacefully, on May 11. The call met with wide support, and thousands of people took to the streets in improvised meetings. The response included an unusual absence from schools, colleges, and universities, noisy protests by car drivers, and disruption of traffic during the night, as burning barricades were thrown up in many parts of the capital by scores of protesters. The sound of empty pots, which a decade earlier had been the symbol of rebellion by middle- and high-income groups against the socialist government of Salvador Allende, was heard again in all the neighborhoods of Santiago.

The broadness of this expression of discontent and the nature of the disturbances in certain areas of the city, despite violent crackdowns, were a clear indication that the population had lost its fear. From this time on, something more than coercion would be necessary to maintain the submission the military desired.

The days of protest were repeated one after the other in the first weeks of each remaining month in 1983 and on at least four more occasions during 1984. The intensity of the political conflict grew rapidly, and the political stability of the Pinochet regime was seriously threatened to such an extent that hundreds of foreign correspondents gathered on a monthly basis in Santiago to report the final downfall of a dictatorship that for a decade had been tragic news across the world. The increasingly widespread character of the civil protest and lack of control of government action appeared as unequivocal signs that such an outcome could come about, bringing Chile in line with the democratic tide sweeping the rest of Latin America.

And yet the hoped-for ending did not occur. On the contrary, after eighteen months of intense mobilization and repression, which led to official figures of 160 dead and 500 with bullet wounds, Chile ended 1984 under a state of siege, with an opposition movement as broad as it was perplexed and increasingly distant from the social forces that supported it. And to complicate the picture further, some surveys carried out at the time showed that a majority of the population—although continuing to hold an outright preference for an immediate change of government and a return to democracy—also supported the declaration of the state of siege.

Two questions must be asked about this singular period in Chilean political history. First, how can the massive, sudden demonstrations that began in May 1983 be explained when, for an entire decade, the opposition to the military regime had been so weak and diffuse? Was it the result of a false step by the military, unforeseeable until that moment? Or was it due to a realignment of the social actors themselves? And second, why did the protest movement not continue to grow, as many observers expected, but rather, having reached a certain point, begin to decline? Was this the result of the cunning behavior of its antagonist (the military dictatorship), or was it attributable to factors intrinsic in the movement itself? In the analysis of this point lies one of the keys to understanding the subsequent reconstruction of the Chilean party system and the peculiar transition to democracy in the country.

With the benefit of a certain historical hindsight, one thing seems certain: the protests had the ability to transform resistance into a non-heroic act but did not manage to articulate a social movement that could serve as an alternative to the authoritarian order and permit a progressive increase in the challenge to the power of the state. Civil society was caught between fear of the state and fear of its own self-destructive tendencies. The depth of national division in the previous era, even given the clear integrative failure of the military's moderniz-ing project, tilted the balance in favor of the status quo. From that point, however, the government of the generals lost all its persuasive capacity over the population: the "no" vote of 1988 against Pinochet's continuing in government was decided in 1983.

## A Form of Nonheroic Resistance

During almost the entire first decade of military government in Chile, manifestations of discontent were rare. They were principally carried out by small, politically active nuclei and met a limited reception within the population. The end of the first period of consolidation of the new government saw a radical policy of repression directed against the political and social organizations that had supported Allende's govern-ment or even those that, in the opinion of the new regime, had been too soft on it. These organizations were replaced by clandestine groups that continually called for an uprising against the new regime and by sectors of the civil population who sought open forms of political response and opposition. Ten years is a long time, and yet neither demonstrations nor sympathy for these groups appeared to grow sig-nificantly. Given this, how does one explain the sudden outbreak of massive demonstrations starting in May 1983?

The phenomenon could certainly be explained away by referring to the drastic contraction in the Chilean economy beginning in the second half of 1981, following the dramatic but false expansion that took place from the end of 1976 to the end of 1980. These two abrupt cycles, of explosive growth followed by a violent fall in output, could be the basis for an interpretation that a massive frustration of the expectations pro-duced by the boom years gave rise to a rebellion in society.

This explanation may be adequate in many respects, but it does not sufficiently distinguish the situation within which the protests came about. Not every situation of massive frustration leads to the same results, and in fact a recessive cycle of similar intensity took place during 1974 and 1975 (immediately after a strong expansion in pur-chasing power of waged workers, in social and political participation, and in a long series of indicators of social modernization during 1964–73), but with opposite results. The way general frustration manifests itself in protest and rebellion and the way actors and script coincide on the stage require a sociopolitical rather than purely economic explanation. If the individual dissatisfactions or frustrations were transformed in 1983 into collective action followed by protest and rebellion, this was because, above and beyond structural conditions, there had been a change among the actors. This can be best described as the overcoming of a "heroic syndrome" in relation to power.

Political repression, combined with police action that extends beyond the public domain and leads to disproportionate punishment, contributes to a vicious circle of fear. This is especially so when repressive measures are carried out in a sustained manner by the state and when they manage to overcome the first line of resistance offered by existing social organizations. From this moment, fear reproduces itself with a progressive growth in the isolation of the groups and individuals who most actively offer resistance to the authoritarian order. This vicious circle was well described some centuries ago by Niccolo Machiavelli in his formulation of "how cities or states should be governed which, before being occupied, operated according to their own rules."[6]

The principal condition for overcoming this vicious circle of fear lies in the rupture of what can be called the "heroic syndrome": a generalized perception on the part of the dominated that they are all equal with regard to their relation to a central and superior power, and that they are all equally defenseless in the face of such power. Resistance to this superior power therefore cannot be suggested in terms of rational-instrumental strategies; it must take the form of an affirmation of a body of superior ethical values that can be demonstrated only by expressive action of an extraordinary type. Given the social equality of weak power resources, such resistance is subject to the unequal interindividual distribution of courage. In this situation the majority of the population adopts the stance of spectator and an individual or small group becomes the hero. Since heroism can only be matched by acts of a similar magnitude of risk, this tends to reinforce the difference between the individual or small group and the masses (who adopt positions of indifference, rejection, or worship).

The Chilean protests of 1983 did overcome the heroic syndrome in terms of at least three factors, which must be examined in order to understand the subsequent decline of the protest movement. These factors are the nature of those who called the protest, the wide range of activities undertaken, and the collective support for these actions.

THOSE CALLING THE PROTEST.  The first "national protest" of May 11, 1983, was called by the Copper Workers Confederation. This is far from being a trivial detail, as it was people's confidence in the strategic importance of this group that, to a large extent, determined the success of the protest call. There had been numerous previous calls to protest, to resist, to strike, and to rebel. This call met a different response because diverse social sectors shared the perception, based on historical experience, that the copper industry was the key to the economy of the country. A halt in its activities could create unmanageable economic problems, which in the past had traditionally forced governments to negotiate.

From a strictly economic point of view, large-scale copper mining, in terms of formal and informal demand, affected approximately 11 percent of the production and distribution chains in the Chilean economy.[7] In financial terms, its importance was much greater since it offered, in the final analysis, the principal security for all public-sector—and indirectly private-sector—loans in the country. The political-professional strike of October 1972 against the Allende regime—which, in the words of then U.S. president Richard Nixon, made the Chilean economy scream—was carried out by a combination of economic sectors whose stoppage affected 15 percent of production and distribution without, at the same time, affecting financial flows. This gives an indication as to why the copper workers are considered so powerful in Chile.

The importance of a call for protest from the CTC cannot, however, simply be reduced to the perception of its strategic importance in the Chilean economy. From the point of view of the very configuration of social actors, it represented a decisive turnaround.

In contrast to ideological interpretations of recent Chilean history (particularly the ideological visions of history emerging during the 1960s and 1970s), which often reduce the trade unions to a single homogeneous movement, politically radical and class-oriented, we can clearly distinguish between at least two broad currents in the union movement. These had different orientations from around the end of World War II. One was a movement based principally in great industrial enterprises and traditional mining, protected from external competition by the state and traditionally in private hands. Given the limited strategic importance of this sector in the national economy and the weakness of the bosses in the face of labor demands at the microeconomic level, this union movement tended to operate principally as a political actor, combining a radical class discourse with the owners and an emphasis on negotiation with the state hierarchy. The battle against the effects of inflation on wage purchasing power led to a long-term alliance of this sector with the workers from public and private bureaucracies, giving rise in 1952 to the Central Union of Workers (CUT). There was another movement, however, that never merged with this one except in a few limited struggles. The other union movement was even more powerful, and it had a more professional than political orientation. It was based in the large strategic state enterprises or foreign-owned industries (copper, electricity, petroleum, ports, and steel). Given its privileged location and the economic strength of the employers, it did not require broad alliances to give weight to its demands but could negotiate directly at the firm level.

A call from the copper workers thus had the result of uniting these two great currents of the union movement. This took place at a time when traditional unionism was in a state of some decline due to the liquidation of its operating base (brought about by the removal of protection for traditional industry and the reduction in public bureaucracy since 1974) and its extreme commitment to the previous regime, which segmented and reduced its persuasive capacity. In contrast, the activist base of the unionism represented by the copper workers had remained largely unaffected by economic policy during the decade and also retained its capacity to link up with middle-class professional organizations.

These economic and social factors were translated, from the very moment of calling the protest, into a rupture of the heroic syndrome that had dominated antiauthoritarian resistance before 1983. In effect, they broke the perception of the equality of impotence of individuals before the state, setting up a strong line of protection that provided protest supporters with security.

THE SCOPE OF THE ACTIONS.  Setting up this line of protection in the call for the first protest allowed a second feature of the heroic syndrome to be overcome. This concerned the situation of equality in the face of power, whereby an ethical demand for expressive action compels individuals or small groups to act in a way that is beyond their ordinary capacity. The existence of a line of protection allows them to act as they really are: individuals or small groups with ordinary capacities. In chess, a pawn can threaten like a bishop but it dies as a pawn. A pawn protected by a bishop can reach the extremes of daring and threaten a king through the small moves it is permitted, one square forward at a time. It is difficult for a heroic pawn to be followed by others unless it is protected. Expressive emotion is displaced by the instrumental rationality of action.

There was nothing heroic in what was being asked in the actions that made up the protests of 1983–84: not to send children to school, not to buy anything or carry out routine business or paperwork, not to use public transport, to stay at home, and to sound car horns at the same time. The people went beyond these actions in various ways during the first protest. But it is interesting to note that this still followed a line of conduct proper to individuals and small groups with ordinary capacities.

Seen in their entirety, the set of protest actions generally advanced the frontiers that separated private from public space and tended toward a progressive domestication of the latter. It is for this reason that the protests can be analyzed from a territorial perspective.

Taking a spatial perspective on the protests, one can see that the mobilizations were made up of a number of actions that rejected the central space of the board (proper to spectacular or heroic action) and attempted to advance from the margins of the private and daily space of each individual. This stretched the forces of repression, leading to their maximum dispersion and considerably reducing the disequilibrium between defenseless individuals or groups and central power. Even when—in some situations—they went beyond the passive forms of resistance called for, the protests therefore managed to overcome the heroic syndrome.

COLLECTIVE SUPPORT.    In contrast to extraordinary forms of behavior, ordinary conduct requires something different if it is to overcome fear. This is the strength that arises from the awareness that many are doing the same or even more and that this conduct is not particularly susceptible to punishment (or at least it does not figure among the main punishable activities). Therefore what is needed is not to be separated from the masses, but rather to be inextricably intertwined with them.

The first type of support necessary for a collective demonstration such as the protests was the certainty that the line of protection continued to be strong. The second was the continued perception that there was a body of people doing more than that asked of the majority. The third was the certainty that the majority were actually doing what was expected of them.

With regard to the protests of 1983 and 1984, a distinction can be drawn between the days before each protest, the actual day of the protest, and the night of the protest. In the days before, the call was repeated and attention drawn to new participants. Sometimes the successful outcome of certain test cases would also strengthen that line (for example, a verdict in the courts against those responsible for repressive violence on previous protests, the freeing of those calling the protest on the basis of lack of a prosecution case, the appearance of a slight relaxation on the part of the regime, or the defense by the church of those who had suffered the most fierce repression). During the actual day of the protest, the combination of the challenge to fear and fear of the protest produced the first visible results: low school attendance, little public transport, little movement in the city, closed shops. On the other hand, the active social and political sector, including students, intellectuals, political militants, and leaders, began demonstrations in various parts of the city (particularly in the center), making it clear that this was no ordinary day and initiating the protest with acts that required more courage than those asked of the rest of the population. During the night the sound of empty pots and horns, neighborhood activity, and news from other parts of the city and country strengthened the perception that the protesters constituted a majority.

These support mechanisms obviously required a fluid network of social communication. Their effectiveness depended upon an up-to-date knowledge of the overall situation with respect to the demonstrations, especially since the great majority took place outside the central areas. Thus the radio stations of the opposition played a crucial role, and the government habitually responded by banning their news service.

### Growth and Stagnation of the Challenge

If overcoming fear of the state was the first condition for the success of the protests, the second was the persistence and growth of their challenge to the power of the state. The existence of a line of protection had, as mentioned above, the effect of replacing expressive emotionality with a certain degree of instrumental rationality. This latter required, however, some evidence of the effectiveness of the actions: that history was not a black hole but at least a tunnel, with progress being made toward the light at the end of it. Growing optimism in relation to the future was a factor of as much importance as the line of protection; and once the first steps had been taken in the challenge to power, its importance became even greater.

The development of the Chilean protests showed at least two stages in relation to this factor. The first, which lasted from the first to the fourth protest, seemed to show a growing challenge to power even when there was no parallel growth in the scope of the actions of the civil population. During the second phase, which began with the fifth protest (September 1983), the movement seemed to be settling into a routine, its social scope becoming more limited, and the actions undertaken subject to a segmented growth in their character and daring.

THE PERIOD OF GROWING CHALLENGE.  It is curious to note that although between May and August 1983 the magnitude of the actions undertaken by the civil population during the days of protest did not really change, the perception of both internal and external observers was that the challenge to the authoritarian regime was becoming ever greater. Furthermore, there was a feeling that the military government was increasingly losing control over the social and political situation in the country. Although it is true that between the first and second days of protests (May 11 and June 11, 1983) there was a notable increase in the scope of the movement (and it continued growing, albeit at a less spectacular rate in the two following months), the real reason for such a perception did not rest with those participating in the protests but with their antagonist.

The lack of control of the military government was, more than anything, a lack of control over its own responses. Police behavior in Santiago had been relatively efficient during the day of the first protest but became more reckless during the night, with the proliferation of protest activities and their more aggressive nature. The fear this provoked in government ranks meant that, beginning the day after the first protest, while the opposition majority were celebrating their newfound unity and the possibilities for the future, the government responded with measures that were far too drastic. This left them few new methods to face the protests over the following months, as they shut down radio stations, announced criminal charges against those who had called the protest, and made massive raids on low-income neighborhoods. The perception that the government had responded in such a disproportionate way could have renewed fear, but the nature of the first great demonstration of collective discontent in ten years stopped this from happening. Indeed, the security felt on discovering this sense of being an active majority allowed another reading of the government's reaction: "If the government responds with high cards then we must hold a very good hand."

On top of this, the repressive response of the government to the first protest was ineffective and vacillating. Despite the government's expectations, nothing significant emerged from the massive raids on low-income neighborhoods in terms of arms, urban guerrillas, or activists who might have instigated the movement. Nearly all the detainees had to be quickly returned to their homes, and the reaction against media censorship (including that of the official media) was of such a level that the government had to lift the decree banning news broadcasts from opposition radio stations. The detention of the leader of the Copper Workers Confederation was resolved when he was freed on bail the next day. The measures taken seemed to reinforce the perception that the protest had triumphed and to reduce fear of participating in a further demonstration of discontent.

This type of disproportionate and clumsy government response continued in the following three months, every one of which was marked by a broader protest. After the second day of protest (June 11), the leader of the CTC was violently detained and held prisoner days before the date announced for the third protest (July 12). Days before the fourth protest, the highest leaders of the Christian Democrat party, the biggest center party in the country, were detained and held incommunicado. During the third and fourth protests, a curfew was declared from midday. For the fourth protest (August 11), the capital city awoke to find itself occupied by 18,000 troops who patrolled the streets in a menacing fashion. The number of victims and detainees grew (especially in the fourth protest). In this way, even though the actions carried out by the population continued to be the same, the repression unleashed by the government expanded at such a rate—even reaching the level of hysteria in August—that it was possible to maintain the perception that the challenge to state power was growing.

Such a perception was sustained in turn by two immediate successes of the movement. Certain political openings developed: there was an increase in authorization for the return of exiles, censorship on books was lifted, and space was created for the appearance of new opposition media. At the same time, the line of protection was defended: the courts ordered the unconditional liberty of the Christian Democrat leaders, arguing that calling for peaceful protests did not constitute a crime. Also released were the leaders of the union coordinating committee who had been detained and, a few days later, the leader of the CTC. These facts served to affirm that the government's inconsistent and inefficient response was one of desperation. This tended to reduce fear and led to a growing confidence that the road chosen was a good one.

Together with the government response, a second factor reducing fear and reinforcing the perception that gains were being made was the increasing breadth of the line of protection. The first protest (May 1983) was called by the CTC. The second protest (June 1983) was called by the nascent National Workers Command (which grouped together the CTC and other union leaderships); the Democratic Workers Union (which grouped the dock workers, white-collar workers, and unionists from strategic sectors such as steel and petroleum); the traditionally moderate Confederation of Chilean Employees; and the union heirs of the CUT and radical workers' tradition, the National Union Coordinator and United Workers Front. The protest appeal was also supported by organizations that brought together old political and business leaders who had been in the first line of struggle against the Allende regime. These included the Project for National Development, professional organizations, and the Supreme Council of Road Transport. It even received support from an ex-member of the military junta (Air Force General Gustavo Leigh, who had been sacked by Pinochet). Various business organizations, while not explicitly supporting the protest, increased their criticisms of the economic policies of the regime and made clear their sympathies for their opponents. The third protest (July 1983), which took place with the leader of the CTC in prison, allowed for the baton to be passed from the corporative organizations (unions and business associations, or *gremios*) to the political parties: the recently formed Democratic Manifesto (a multiparty grouping made up of the Christian Democrat, Socialist, Radical, Social-Democrat and Republican right parties) was in charge of convoking the protest, and this was supported by those who had previously called for such actions.

By June 1983, therefore, a new sociopolitical majority had formed in the country, overcoming for the first time in ten years the lines of division of the Popular Unity period, which had separated the center from the left, the unionism of the large company from more traditional unions, and the latter from small business *gremios*. The perception was of a new alignment that would finally leave behind the trauma of polarization at the beginning of the 1970s and close the entranceway to the tunnel of dictatorship. Perhaps this was the moment in which the civil population felt the least fear, as it observed the clear impotence of authoritarian control and the fact that the phantom of ungovernability was receding. For this reason, the demonstrations of July 12 and August 11–12 represented the highest point of antiauthoritarian mobilization.

ROUTINE AND DISENCHANTMENT.  The two dimensions that came to-gether to produce a change in the limit of fear (overcoming the heroic syndrome and encouraging the perception of achievement) depended on factors that were nevertheless changing during the first four months of antiauthoritarian mobilization. The effects of these changes made themselves felt at the turning point of August 1983. Reaching the point of maximum pressure, the political and social actors found it necessary to move another piece in order to place the regime "in check" and open the road to democratization. It was a moment of calculation and tactics now that certain psychosocial factors impeding the protests had been removed.

The force that initially set up the line of protection in the face of fear was the threat of a strike in the copper mines. The first call of the CTC in April 1983 had been for a national strike and not a protest movement. The protest was decided on as a replacement for the strike only two days before the date set, owing to the problems other union centers had in mobilizing their rank and file around an objective as momentous as stopping work. Despite this, the specter of a political national strike remained, during the first two protests, as a probable next step. There-fore it retained its immediacy in the expectations of the majority who supported the demonstrations—giving them the nature of a show of force with a possible recourse to the original plan. On the other hand, the eventual move from a strike to a protest allowed the convergence of the most powerful segment of trade unionism with the two biggest social categories in the country: the middle classes and the marginal-ized or excluded groups.

On May 26, 1983, the president of the CTC was detained on the orders of the Pinochet government. Complying with a previous agree-ment to escalate to strike action if reprisals were taken against its leaders, the CTC met to study this course of action. Their leader was, however, quickly freed on bail by the courts and a strike did not come about.

On June 15, the same leader was violently arrested and this time the confederation responded with an immediate strike call, which came into effect the following day. In contrast to the protests, this call was directed only at the copper workers, and the CTC faced an important test of its strength. The strike call met a wide response among workers in three out of five areas (large mines) but met obstacles in the two remaining areas and among administrative workers. The state company CODELCO decreed the immediate dismissal of 1,800 workers and invited interested people to apply for the vacant posts. Large queues of unemployed workers formed at the company, and this harmed the strike in areas that had not yet voted. Seven days after the CTC strike call, when this strike had already been broken by the company, the transport workers called for a strike of truck owners, which took place between June 23 and 24 without having a profound impact on public opinion due to the prevailing censorship. The possibility of uniting both forces had ceased to exist, and the transport workers ended their strike on June 25 after achieving an acceptable negotiated settlement to their sectoral grievances with the government.

From this point on, the entropic tendency inside the CTC, which in the past had kept it apart from the rest of the union movement, began to reestablish itself. Much the same happened with the associations of transport workers. The role of the political parties in calling the protest in June reestablished the potency of the national movement for democracy and maintained intact the line of protection against fear for the population. Nevertheless, the principal material force of the movement had been dented.

The strength of the political parties lay in their broad capacity for national mobilization, but this was much more symbolic than material. This was also true for most of the union centers apart from the CTC. The clear impotence of the military's modernizing project at the time meant that, unlike the situation in other countries such as Brazil, there were no new social groups strategically inserted in the occupational structure. On the contrary, there was a growing weakening and decomposition of existing groups. The inorganic nature of the structure of employment (see chapters 2 and 4) conspired against the capacity of the actors to mobilize tactically in a disciplined way at crucial moments. Between 1971 and 1982, the share of waged workers in the active population had fallen from 53 percent to 38 percent. During the same period, those excluded from formal employment rose from 14 percent of the labor force to 36 percent. Among youth, the principal base for mobilization in the protests, exclusion reached 70 percent.[8]

Among the associations of the middle classes, on the other hand, the withdrawal of the transport organizations (already announced for the

August protest) left professional and commercial sectors isolated from a fundamental ally.

The tactical options available to the principal actors of the political, union, and *gremio* world after the peak of August 1983 could have been the incorporation of the movement into semi-institutional channels, increasing routinization of the protests (that is, their continuation without the possibility of extending the challenge to power), or an insurrectional movement of the urban masses. From September 1983, the protests were systematically reduced in scope until the beginning of new and brief cycles in March–April and September–October 1984. Important advances had been made and fear of the state had been reduced. It had been replaced, however, with growing disenchantment.

## Disintegrating Tendencies and Fear of Society

The realignment of June 1983 was short-lived. In fact, the conditions for its extinction were growing even as it was born. During the first protest, in May, it had been possible to observe a difference in the character and magnitude of the mobilizations among different social sectors of the city. Between the second and fourth protests, there was growing social segmentation of the activities, with the eruption of violence, principally in the low-income neighborhoods. These showdowns with the police took on considerable dimensions and were sometimes accompanied by pillage and vandalism inside the liberated zones, actions seized upon by the official press. The line between political protest and criminal activity was often difficult to draw, particularly among the young. It would be better to say that both were manifestations of a radical rejection of a social order that excluded and oppressed them. Violent conduct often went much further than battling the police and extended to looting shops, burning buses, and extorting money from drivers and pedestrians. The free space opened by the protests allowed for the liberation of a wide body of energy and frustrations. It was difficult to subject these to the simple logic of the accumulation of political strength.

On the other hand, there was also a sharp social divide in terms of the level of repression. In the popular neighborhoods this was very brutal, while fewer resources and personnel were dedicated to high- and middle-income neighborhoods. The spiral of violence can be looked at from a different perspective than that which is commonly adopted. Owing to the brutality of police action, there was a very aggressive response from the youth who lived in conditions of extreme disintegration and anomie. By labeling them violent, the police helped to make them so. Whichever way it is seen, this factor helped to weaken the interclass solidarity that had been so arduously constructed by the democratic movement.

To this must be added a paradoxical effect of the emergence of the "line of protection." This was made up of actors who were relatively central to the political and economic system. The centrality of the actors is frequently linked to their closeness to positions not only of power but also of prestige, honor, and privilege. This, while inducing trust, also makes them the object of resentment. In a country as politically polarized as Chile, the great majority of those calling the protest and forming the line of protection came from the sectors most militantly opposed to Popular Unity and President Allende, whose symbolic importance was still intact in the popular sectors despite the attempts made by official propaganda to wipe it out. The paradoxical effect arises, therefore, from the fact that the line of protection also led to the demand for their own identity by the political and social sectors that had suffered the longest and most systematic persecution during the first decade of military rule. If one takes into account the fact that even the symbolic actions calling for protest (the banging of pots and sounding of horns) had their origins in anti-Allende protests, plus the much greater susceptibility of the marginal areas to repression, one can understand the profundity of the demand for identity, autonomy, and differentiation.

At the same time, the growing violence in marginal areas, the more intensive use of *allendista* symbols by the demonstrators, and the open resentment shown in these areas toward the leaders and tactics of the middle class all led to a growing terror on the part of the middle class. There was fear of polarization and the dictatorship of the masses, against which the middle class had risen up only a decade earlier. The growing social segmentation of the protests became the mechanism through which fear of the state returned to one of its original sources: civil society's fear of its own self-destructive tendencies.

The tragedy of the Chilean protest movement manifested itself most clearly in August 1983. Instead of attempting to use the social and political realignment of June to rechannel the effects of social division into a new form of political expression, the movement sought to represent that division in the political arena. On August 7, 1983, four days before the biggest challenge to the authoritarian regime, the Democratic Alliance was established. This was made up of the parties who were signatories to the Democratic Manifesto (Christian Democrat, Radical, the majority section of the Socialist party, and other small parties). Its first act was to support the call for a protest on August 11 and 12, which had been made by different sectors. On August 25, the majority of the parties in the alliance began a series of dialogue meetings with the government, which was represented by its new minister of the interior. A few days later, however, a second group, the Popular Democratic Movement, was set up (composed of the Communist party, the Movement of the Revolutionary Left, factions of the Socialist party, and other small parties). Its first public expression was a categorical rejection of the dialogue with the government carried out by the Democratic Alliance. From that moment, there was an explicit difference of orientation between a semi-institutional opposition (preferring dialogue, authorized marches and demonstrations, judicial battles, and acquisition of influence and control over legal or semilegal social organizations) and a semi-insurrectional opposition (preferring to form militias, engage in assassination attempts, and take part in local strikes). Between the two the only point of contact was the sporadic repetition of routine protests.

In consequence, the protests of 1983 (and not those of 1984) must be analyzed as movements that could have overcome the social and political division of 1973 but failed to do so. This was the essential condition for relegitimizing politics, and thus the failure of the protests also discredited politics for the majority of the population. If the coup of 1973 has been offered as a classic example of the Marxist theory of the state—in which the armed forces appear as the defenders of the interests of the dominant class—then the Chilean protests of 1983–84 would have to be identified as a classic example of Hobbesian theory. The persistence of a military dictatorship, far from simply being a question of the relationship between civilians and the military, came to be explained by the nature of the relations of fear and mistrust among civilians themselves.

## Democratization

The military government concentrated particularly on dealing with the economic aspects of the crisis of 1983. This may have been due to its erroneous diagnosis of the protests solely as a reaction to the severe recession affecting the national economy, or because it could do little else, given its lack of an effective plan for political and institutional normalization. This economistic outlook had already been dominant among the ideologues of the regime since they overcame the previous recessive cycle (1974–77). The official technocracy maintained the expectation of an effective transition toward a democracy "protected" by the armed forces and founded on "a country of property owners and not proletarians," in General Pinochet's own words. It was accepted that an increase in consumption levels, the extension of private property, and reduction in the size of the state would automatically create the conditions for a stable democracy that excluded the political left. Such confidence was shown to be completely naive in the light of post-1983 developments.

From 1984, through the application of a series of corrective measures to economic policy, principally to exchange rate strategy, the Chilean economy began a vigorous recovery. Nevertheless, this process did not lead in any way to an increase in levels of support for the regime. Political opinion polls, which were carried out in greater freedom from 1985 onward, clearly illustrate this point: declared support for General Pinochet never exceeded 30 percent of the samples interviewed, while the desire for a change of government and speedy return to democracy systematically exceeded 45 percent of responses.[9] These surveys cannot be compared with similar studies carried out before the events of 1983 (because such studies were not authorized, and those who managed to carry them out could do so only in suboptimal methodological conditions). Therefore it is not possible to confirm with empirical evidence that the military government had lost support during the years of economic crisis and social protests (unless the disputed figures of the 1978 and 1980 plebiscites are taken as a base). It is, however, certain that the military government did not gain support from the population as a result of economic recovery.

The general perception of the population was that the military government had no desire to advance toward any form of democratic transition, but simply aspired to remain perpetually in power. For a "transition from above" to take place, the military government would have had to take consistent steps to open up a competitive arena for political representation, recognizing a reality that would not be altered from 1983 onward: the reconstitution of the political parties as well as union, student, and professional organizations. These not only expressed themselves publicly and enjoyed solid support from the population but had even been recognized at the height of the crisis by the government itself, as it engaged in "dialogue" to find solutions to the political crisis.

But as social mobilization through the protests began to decrease in intensity, the military government discarded this course of action and accepted the resignation of the veteran right-wing political leader, Sergio Onofre Jarpa, as minister of the interior. He had been appointed to this position by Pinochet with the very objective of initiating a dialogue with the opposition at the most critical moment of the crisis. Once again, the government's conduct gave clear signals of its aspiration to cling to the personal concentration of power rather than to advance toward some form of political opening.

"Dictatorships are like bicycles: when they stop moving, they fall." This phrase, attributed to the Spanish ideologue José Antonio Primo de Rivera, is remarkably appropriate for describing the fate of the supposed "political plan" of the Chilean military government. Throughout the years of mobilization and protest, the only constant factor that appeared to guide its action was that of arriving at the 1988 plebiscite and finding a new source of Caesarist legitimacy. And although the reality of events pointed urgently to the need to modify the timetable for institutional change, the only possible source of consensus within the power bloc (and in particular among the armed forces) on how to achieve this without affecting the concentration of power in the hands of the commander-in-chief of the army was to adhere strictly to the calendar set out in the 1980 constitution. The constitutional norm became a source of both strength and weakness for General Pinochet. His base of support fully accepted that he would stay in power until 1988, as set out in the constitution approved in 1980. At the same time, his supporters kept their distance with respect to his staying in power after that date and started to perceive him as an obstacle to the social and economic stability of the country. The well-known fable with which Wilfred Pareto illustrated his theory of elite circulation holds true again: once the emergency that brought the "lions" to power has receded, they begin to be replaced by "foxes."[10]

The first signs of a growing autonomy of the political right with respect to the military government came a little after the exit of their veteran leader from the Interior Ministry. Party currents appeared that sought to represent the base of the old National party. Organizations such as National Unity, National Work Front, and the Independent Democratic Union all made their public appearance in 1985, with the aim of politically supporting the government and "continuing its work" after 1988. Although their discourse was of frank support for General Pinochet and his government, the fact that they had their own autonomous constitution after twelve years of recognizing military leadership (following their self-dissolution after the 1973 coup) represented a clear message of independence.

The Catholic Church also changed its political role during the upheaval of 1983. Institutionally, the Vicariate of Solidarity, and the multiple initiatives it had supported, continued in the defense of human rights. Its objective, however, following the replacement of the archbishop of Santiago by a more conservative successor, was now based on the creation of dialogue and understanding between the forces of the political opposition and the principal civilian supporters of the regime. The testimonial opposition of Cardinal Raúl Silva Henríquez gave way to the diplomatic efforts of Cardinal Juan Francisco Fresno, in tune with new tendencies in the Vatican. The appearance on the scene of the opposition political parties favored this change of profile.

The evolution of the political opposition after two years of the protest movement reflected the definitive separation of the two roads that had emerged at the peak of the protests. The first sought to create the political conditions for a negotiated transition between the civilian forces of the opposition and those supporting the military government. It was headed by a broad coalition of parties, whose center of gravity was the understanding between the Socialist party and the Christian Democrats. The second was based around the Communist party and directed toward the overthrow of the military regime by revolutionary methods.

The revolutionary road arrived somewhat overdue and had a brief life. For almost three decades, the Chilean Communist party had been a model of reformist politics and had systematically opposed, in its relations with left-wing allies, revolutionary positions that it considered to be both inadequate for the "national anti-oligarchic transformation," as established in its program, and politically isolationist. Using the same criteria, the party analyzed the Popular Unity experience and the reasons for its defeat.[11] This led it to put forward the idea in late 1973 of building a "broad front against fascism," with the objective of restoring democracy. The front would be based on an alliance between the parties of Popular Unity and the Christian Democrats, united in opposition to the Pinochet dictatorship. This approach was replaced by the strategy of "popular rebellion"—theoretically at first, around the middle of

1979, and in practice toward the end of 1983 (with the setting up of an armed organization, the Manuel Rodríguez Patriotic Front, or FPMR).

This revolutionary policy attempted to continue the insurrectional road once the protest movement entered its decline toward the middle of 1984. In contrast to the national movement, however, it attempted to radicalize the forms of challenge to the military regime, resorting to ever more specialized and violent forms of struggle that in turn contributed to the ebb of such massive mobilizations. Two events in 1986 demonstrated the definitive distancing of this policy from the democratic movement and destroyed its capacity to offer an initiative. The first was the discovery by the security services of a substantial arsenal of weapons that the FPMR was attempting to bring into the country through a small fishing port in the north of the country. The second was the "flight forward" by the FPMR, a month after the frustration of that episode, with the failed attempt to kill General Pinochet. Both actions led to a recovery of the leadership capacity of Pinochet and the security services within the power bloc and to a temporary withdrawal of support by the population—fearful of a violent outcome—for the opposition to the authoritarian regime.

It is strange to note that in contrast to this change in the Communist party an exactly opposite change took place at the heart of the Socialist party and the "new left" in general, both of which had been exponents of revolutionary transformation until after the fall of Allende. This change grew out of a critique of socialism, assuming a democratic objective, and led to a process of "renovation" of a social democratic nature. Such a process of socialist renovation was, in turn, a precondition for the constitution of the alliance that would head the democratic movement and lead to the transition to democracy. The changes within the center-left required to overcome the origins of the 1973 crisis did not come from the antifascist front outlined by the Communist party, but rather from an understanding between renovated socialists and the Christian Democrat leadership emerging in 1983 and headed by those sectors within the party that had been most critical of military intervention.

Throughout the period of intense social mobilization, the political road of opposition to the regime consisted basically of overcoming three challenges. The first was the organization of the majority participating in the protests, reestablishing the historic ties of party representation and giving them a unified tactical direction. The second was the construction of relations with the civil forces that supported the military regime, bringing about a nonconfrontational political arena for the replacement of authoritarian decisionmaking. The third was the transformation of the 1988 plebiscite from a ritual of Caesarist legitimation into an opportunity for peaceful change and effective transition toward a democratic regime.

The changes that were taking place on the political right as well as the change in the political profile of the Catholic Church facilitated the first effort to overcome military involvement in political relations among civilians. In August 1985, on the initiative of the church of Santiago, a meeting took place for the first time between personalities representing a wide range of political currents (from regime supporters to representatives of groups that had made up Popular Unity) in order to debate the transition to democracy. The meeting ended with the signing of a "National Accord for the Transition to Full Democracy." This was an important symbolic milestone within the new political phase that was opening. Although the document did not contain any agreement that would change the timetable of institutionalization set out in the constitution of 1980, it did mark the possibility for a new basic consensus that would end the recent exceptional political years. The national accord was to mark the beginning of subsequent meetings that tended to reestablish the basic solidarities of the political class, profoundly weakened since 1973.

The establishment of a common tactical direction in the democratic opposition—which had its immediate predecessor in the Democratic Alliance set up in 1983—was favored by the 1988 plebiscite. The Democratic Alliance had been based on an understanding between modernizing factions—until then, in the majority—of the Christian Democrat and Socialist parties. But the decline in the protest movement in 1984 was accompanied by a radicalization of party bases that strengthened the most uncompromising sectors. The decision to participate in the plebiscite of 1988 therefore came at a time when the alliance and its modernizing center were losing ground to "traditional" extremes (expressing the historic reluctance of the Christian Democrats to form alliances and the orthodox leftism of the Socialist party). The path represented by the plebiscite, however, reduced the importance of these differences. All that was required was a simple "no" to Pinochet, without the immediate necessity to produce a common alternative government program. From the Democratic Alliance, the political opposition evolved into the coalition for a "no" vote in the plebiscite of 1988.

The mobilization for the "no" became the most important social movement in the country since the first protests of 1983. As in the protests, the principal adversary was the fear of regime repression, and there was a similar necessity to overcome the heroic syndrome and replace it with an aggregation of small gestures that could be made by the entire population. In contrast to the protests, however, the plebiscite actually permitted an institutional outcome for the massive expression of discontent. If the candidate of the military junta did not achieve majority support among the population, there would have to be open elections in a period of not more than a year. In this way, dissident behavior could not only increase but also see the possibility of a successful outcome. This was exactly the balance between change and order that the democratic movement had not managed to achieve by itself during the mobilizations of 1983–84.

The results are well known. An intense opposition mobilization during 1987–88 managed to convince the vast majority of citizens to register to vote, despite the universal suspicion of manipulation and fraud. A variety of opposition parties were registered as well, in spite of the high levels of affiliation demanded of them by the military junta as a requirement for registration. This was a critical step toward ensuring adequate supervision of the ballot in all the voting centers of the country. Finally, the "no" was given a positive and hopeful content in order to establish an atmosphere in which the peaceful transition to democracy would be possible. On October 5, 1988, on the proposal of the military junta that General Augusto Pinochet remain president for a further eight years, the "no" alternative obtained 56 percent of the vote against 44 percent for the "yes." The civil forces supporting the regime immediately recognized the opposition triumph, as did the commander-in-chief of the air force. The government had to do the same hours later.

The coalition for a "no" opened the way for a long-term understanding among the parties that had supported it, becoming the Coalition for Democracy. A body of eighty constitutional reforms was approved in a plebiscite the following year through a consensus arrived at among the Coalition for Democracy, the civilian political forces that had supported the regime, and the government's Interior Ministry. Toward the end of 1989, a new government headed by the coalition emerged triumphant from the polls. It achieved an absolute majority in the Chamber of Deputies and an important representation in the Senate (which re-

mained partially made up of senators designated by the previous regime, according to the constitutional reform agreed to in 1989). The
democratization of the country finally began after sixteen years of dictatorship. And in contrast to other Latin American political transitions,
it did so in a favorable economic climate.

# 2

## The Economy: From the State to the Market

Between 1964 and 1990, the structural and institutional bases of the Chilean economy were radically and irreversibly changed. The transition over this quarter of a century was both rapid and traumatic. In the middle of the 1960s, Chile had a relatively closed economy that depended principally on the copper export enclave, with a restricted number of markets. The state sector was large and controlled an extensive network of public firms, the agricultural sector was backward, and industrial dynamism was concentrated principally in metallurgy. Twenty-five years later, the situation was very different. Chile had an open economy with extended and developed markets. The public sector was leaner and focused on macroeconomic management and regulation. Few state companies existed (although the CODELCO copper company, a mega-firm that had been nationalized in 1971, remained in public ownership). The agricultural sector had become far more advanced, principally through exporting fruit products, while industrial dynamism was largely concentrated in the processing of natural resources. Much more emphasis was placed on a diversified export base (90 percent concentrated in minerals, forestry, fishing, and fruit and 10 percent in manufacturing).

Over these twenty-five years, therefore, the Chilean economic landscape completely changed. Although it continues to be a small economy, dependent on abundant natural resources, its sectoral and spatial structure is very different, as are its economic institutions. Not only has the state's relationship to the economy been transformed, but great changes have taken place in market structures, firms, and the workplace.

41

There is no doubt that during these twenty-five years, long-term secular processes also led to visible changes in the country. The population increased from 8 million to 13 million, urbanization from 72 percent to 82 percent, and average education from five to eight years. Transport and communications networks grew, integrating what had previously been distant and inaccessible areas. Yet Chile was far from experiencing the type of inexorable change that took place in the postwar period in Australia and New Zealand, in Brazil between 1960 and 1980, or in the United States between 1880 and 1910. It did not receive huge numbers of immigrants, and there was no conquest of new territories—not even of new agricultural lands—after this process had been completed in the 1930s.

## The State and Elites

The transformations did not come about as a result of rapid capitalist expansion, dissolving and transforming everything in its path and led by a highly dynamic bourgeoisie. Neither were they particularly due to a cultural atmosphere favorable to such changes. Although there are signs that this process is now beginning to take place during the 1990s, such was not the case during 1964–90. The average growth of GDP was relatively low during this quarter of a century, when compared with other historical periods, and was subject to wide fluctuations (see figure 2-1). Likewise, in the 1970s the Chilean business class was not very dynamic. Although one cannot label it simply as traditional and backward, it is clear that the business class had been sleeping for too long in the shade afforded by state protection and barriers to international competition. Finally, the institutions and culture prevalent during these years were far from favoring the road that the country took from the middle of the 1970s.

In other words, it was not a case of slow and inexorable structural changes that eroded the existing institutions until they finally collapsed. In Chile the reverse was true. Over this quarter of a century radical institutional changes took place that led to the very rapid destruction and re-creation of the social and economic fabric. Simultaneous processes took place with the dismantling of old structures (for example, in the deindustrializing period of 1973–83) and the creation of new ones (for example, the new export model), as well as the dissolution of entire social groups (such as the landowning oligarchy) and the emergence of others (the new economic groups).

FIGURE 2-1. *Per Capita GDP, 1970–95*

1970 = 100

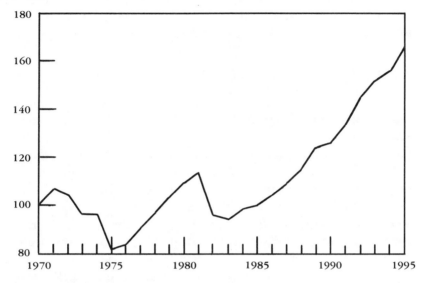

Sources: Central Bank of Chile; National Statistical Institute of Chile.

Our argument is that nearly a decade of progressive reforms (1964–73) and a little more than fifteen years of neoliberal or "free-market" reforms (1973–90) were led not by markets or civil society, but rather by the state and by elites firmly rooted in it. It is striking that although the reforms of 1964–73 had a totally different orientation from those that were imposed in 1973–90, there is a certain continuity between both periods. The economy may have been given its definitive shape during the years of authoritarian rule (1973–90), yet the speed and scope of the reforms were due not only to the power of the state but also to the fact that civil society and the economy were in a very malleable condition.

It could be said that for nearly a quarter of a century it was politics that shaped the economy, although the economy still proceeded to change according to its own gradual dynamic. In the 1990s, a reverse process took place, with the economy becoming more independent from the state and even from politics, although politics also continued to develop following their own logic. The Chile that is the object of study in this book is not one that emerged from inexorable global processes, nor through some overall development process. Instead it is a country transformed by drastic changes in the relationship between state and economy, in market regulations, and even at the micro level in the power relations in factories and between different economic agents. The history of this change began in 1964, but its real genesis was between 1973 and 1990. This is the time period upon which we focus.

## Rupture and Continuity, 1964–90

The neoliberal reforms were mostly imposed on Chilean society by technocratic and military elites, protected by the authoritarian regime. They were actively supported by the business class and passively supported by important sectors of the middle classes. Carried out under the aegis of an authoritarian regime, these reforms promoted a model of political economy anticipating that of the Thatcher government in England, as well as that of the International Monetary Fund and World Bank during the Latin American debt crisis of the 1980s. The radical and durable nature of Chilean neoliberalism is an important historical phenomenon, not just because the right-wing elite adopted an extreme and radical ideology, but because it maintained this position—with some adjustments—in spite of the fact that the authoritarian regime entered a crisis phase after 1983, began to be dismantled after 1988, and was finally replaced by a democratically elected government in 1990.

It might at first sight appear as if the events that took place between 1973 and 1990 were the sole work of those who governed the country during these seventeen years. But no type of economic change, however abrupt it might be, can take place outside the limits and possibilities imposed by historical legacy. What was achieved during 1973–90 was possible not just because of the dictatorial context but also because the progressive reforms that had preceded it, carried out by the democratic governments of Frei and Allende, were also radical and, in some cases, irreversible. This was the case with agrarian reform and the nationalization of copper.

During the decade before the Pinochet regime, there were two democratic governments with very substantial programs for change. The first was the Christian Democrat government of Eduardo Frei Montalva (1964–70), which began the agrarian reform, introduced the partial nationalization ("Chileanization") of copper, and encouraged Latin American economic integration. The second was the government of Salvador Allende (1970–73), which headed a coalition of left-wing parties that had triumphed legitimately at the polls and was committed to initiating a transition from capitalism to socialism. This government undertook changes that radicalized the Frei reforms by increasing agrarian reform and completely nationalizing copper and iron ore. It also introduced new reforms such as the nationalization of the banking system, as well as state intervention in large private companies.

Thus during 1964–73 and in the midst of great social and political confrontations, a series of increasingly left-wing economic reforms were introduced that confiscated the property of the mining transnationals and the landed oligarchy. But this had more far-reaching effects: it weakened the economic power of the national business class while leaving their political power intact so that they could mobilize through their business associations and right-wing political parties. In a situation of deep economic crisis, the business sector gave broad and total support to the new military government, which greatly increased the degree of freedom enjoyed by the technocracy espousing free-market reforms after 1973. In fact, this is what distinguishes Chile from Uruguay and Argentina, where the political and economic weight of the business class remained very important even after the coups of the 1970s, and the military did not enjoy the same degree of autonomy.

## The Background of Free-Market Reform in Chile

It is important to focus not only on the discourse but also the reality of neoliberalism as it existed in Chile. The doctrine afforded a central place to market forces, yet at the end of 1973 there was no part of the economy that was not directly or indirectly managed by the state. In spite of its crisis and disorganization, the state remained crucial to the functioning of the Chilean economy. When the military took power, there were no alternative institutions or economic agents. Previous reforms and recent radical political and social confrontations had left markets in such disarray that they were either manipulated, distorted, or nonexistent.

This produced a strange situation, although one that is not historically uncommon. Given the defeat of popular movements and of the left, as well as the weakness of the business class and markets, the relative power of the state, controlled by the military and the neoliberal technocracy, increased considerably. This elite possessed a rationalizing discourse, had no previous corporate links—although this did not impede them from acquiring such links over the years—and enjoyed

TABLE 2-1. *Basic Economic Indicators, Selected Years, 1974–95*

| Indicator | 1974 | 1977 | 1980 | 1983 | 1986 | 1989 | 1992 | 1995 |
|---|---|---|---|---|---|---|---|---|
| Population (1974 = 100) | 100.0 | 104.7 | 109.5 | 114.7 | 120.4 | 126.5 | 133.1 | 139.6 |
| Total GDP (1974 = 100) | 100.0 | 99.9 | 126.2 | 113.6 | 131.8 | 165.5 | 203.7 | 244.0 |
| Per capita GDP (1974 = 100) | 100.0 | 95.4 | 115.2 | 99.1 | 109.5 | 130.8 | 153.0 | 174.7 |
| Investment (percent of GDP) | 17.4 | 13.3 | 16.6 | 12.0 | 18.9 | 26.0 | 28.2 | 30.7 |
| Public expenditure (percent of GDP) | 32.4 | 24.9 | 23.1 | 28.4 | 30.0 | 29.5 | 23.5 | 22.5 |
| Unemployment rate (percent of labor force) | 10.8 | 11.8 | 10.4 | 19.1 | 8.8 | 5.3 | 4.4 | 4.7 |
| Emergency employment program (percent of labor force) | 0.0 | 5.3 | 5.4 | 13.3 | 0.4 | 0.0 | 0.0 | 0.0 |
| Annual inflation rate (percent) | 375.9 | 63.4 | 31.2 | 23.1 | 17.4 | 21.4 | 12.7 | 8.2 |
| Average real wage (1974 = 100) | 100.0 | 113.9 | 138.2 | 135.1 | 143.2 | 155.1 | 173.1 | 195.0 |
| Average minimum wage (1974 = 100) | 100.0 | 93.4 | 110.4 | 97.1 | 83.6 | 106.3 | 127.0 | 91.2 |

SOURCE: Central Bank of Chile; National Statistical Institute of Chile.

considerable social and business support. Moreover, there were no limits on the use and abuse of force. Thus it was possible to begin a process of structural reforms whose initial trigger was the economic "shock" plan of April 1975, a plan that was neither devised nor imposed by the IMF or the World Bank. Over time, the elite gained experience, expanded its field of activity, and, after the crisis of 1982–83, went from an orthodox monetary approach to a more heterodox one, this time devised and imposed by the IMF and the World Bank.

## The Main Phases of Political Economy, 1973–90

Between 1973 and 1990, Chile experienced a profound restructuring of its productive system, imposed by military and technocratic elites who shared a common project for change and a free-market or neo-liberal ideology in its most extreme form. These changes and their consequences can be separated into two decades. The first, between 1973 and 1983, was characterized by the destruction of the existing socioeconomic fabric. The second was characterized by the creation of new socioeconomic networks that took shape around the end of the 1980s. This restructuring process affected the various sectors of the economy in different ways and at a different pace, but it was particularly intense in agriculture and industry.

The first stage of economic change was marked by structural reforms toward a more open economy, the second by measures to create export-based development. There are similarities between both stages, but the fundamental difference lies in the fact that the first was a foundational period, while the second was dedicated to fine-tuning and adjusting the model. In contrast to the first period, the second included protection for traded goods whose export was supported by tariff and exchange rate policies that favored exporting companies. This was not a permanent feature, however, since after 1990 the degree of opening increased via the reduction of tariffs and real exchange rates, the establishment of multilateral trade agreements (GATT in 1994), and bilateral accords with Mexico, Colombia, and Argentina.

### Structural Reforms to Create an Open Economy

The first phase of reform, from 1973 to 1983, was marked by two massive recessions (1974–75 and 1982–83), as table 2-1 clearly illustrates. This was the period of structural change that would lead to the creation of an open economy. The system of regulations protecting a closed economy with a copper export enclave was dismantled. Three major reforms were rapidly initiated. First, there was a commercial opening through the wholesale reduction of high tariff barriers. Second, state controls, especially in strategic markets (such as the financial market) were dismantled. Third, the first wave of privatizations, which affected profitable public companies, got under way. Although there were similar changes in Argentina and Uruguay, those in Chile were more radical and were not reversed in the 1980s. They also took place within the context of easy access to credit: private external debt multiplied ten times between 1976 and 1981. Tariffs were reduced from an average of 105 percent in 1973 to 10 percent in 1980, at the same time that the peso became increasingly overvalued. This caused a rapid increase in imports, which quadrupled between 1975 and 1981, while exports grew at a much lower rate. This led in turn to a growing balance of payments deficit, although not fiscal deficits. Such a sudden increase in imports, without a corresponding export stimulus, unleashed a major deindustrialization and rationalization of Chilean industry. When this was combined with a drastic reduction in public employment, the high rates of unemployment already associated with the 1974–75 recession began to climb still higher.

## Structural Adjustment: Toward an Export-Based Economy

The second phase, from 1983 to 1990, began with an external debt crisis and developed into a period of structural adjustment leading to the creation of an export-based economy. This took place in tandem with an economic recovery that would lead to renewed expansion after 1988. A broad range of reforms were undertaken in order to consolidate the market system and "subsidiary" state and at the same time adjust the open economy model, which had led to growing external debt and had plunged the country into crisis between 1982 and 1983. One of the most important shifts in policy during the post-1983 period involved the decision to impose tight state regulation on "strategic" markets (interest rates, exchange rates, minimum wages, agricultural prices, and public tariffs) in order to stimulate a structural modification of relative prices that would favor an export economy. The government introduced a series of devaluations that led to a rise in the real exchange rate. It also permitted tariffs to rise from 10 percent in 1982 to an average of 25 percent in 1985, falling back to 15 percent in 1990. This protection allowed the agricultural and industrial sectors some margin for recovery, and they grew at rates higher than 6 percent between 1983 and 1990.

At the same time, there was a further wave of privatizations, as part of the agreement with the IMF and World Bank to improve the fiscal capacity of the Chilean state, which was under strain as it attempted to rescue the country's crisis-ridden banking sector. These privatizations involved public services such as telephones and electricity. Unlike the situation that marked reform in the capital and exchange rate markets, however, few regulatory mechanisms were established in this process of privatization. The result was a concentration of profit in relatively few hands and the emergence of new economic groups. The government also continued with the reform of social security, with the aim of freeing up large amounts of capital for private use (currently social security funds represent 40 percent of GDP). The same process took place in the health system, where the most profitable sectors were privatized. Finally, earlier labor reforms were consolidated in a way that led to a highly flexible use of labor and extremely restricted opportunities for trade union activity. Economic recovery led to a rapid decline in the rate of unemployment, which fell to less than 6 percent in 1990.

## Principal Neoliberal Reforms, 1973–90

Table 2-2 summarizes changes in economic policy in terms of eight principal modifications. These include foreign trade policy, price control or regulation, public ownership, fiscal policy, interest rate policy, capital controls, labor policy, land markets, and social security funds. The following discussion will provide further information on each area of reform and establish the basis for a more analytical discussion in the remainder of the chapter.

### Trade Liberalization

The Chilean economy at the end of 1973 combined a high level of protection with dependence on one principal export (copper). There were multiple exchange rates and a generalized system of quotas, and tariffs ranged from an average of 105 percent to a maximum of 220 percent, reaching their highest level for consumer durables and their lowest for industrial inputs. In addition, imports required "prior deposits." In short, it was an extremely complex system that had developed piecemeal over time. Between 1973 and 1983, within the context of reforms designed to open the Chilean economy, changes in trade

Table 2-2. *Phases of Neoliberal Economic Policy, 1973-90*

| Basic reform | 1973: The end of the Popular Unity government | 1973–82: Toward an open economy | 1983–90: Toward an export economy |
|---|---|---|---|
| Foreign trade | Multiple exchange rates, import quotas; high tariffs (average 105 percent, maximum 220 percent); previous import deposits; trade deficit | Single exchange rate; fixed tariff of 10 percent (not cars); no other barriers; withdrawal from Andean Pact, trade deficit | Single exchange rate; tariffs rise to 25 percent in 1985, fall to 15 percent in 1990; no other barriers; trade surplus from 1985 |
| Prices | General price control; little influence on relative prices | Free prices; between 1974–75, 3,000 controls lifted; fixed tariffs and exchange rate (1979–82); indexed wages | Free prices and wages; indexed tariffs and fixed devaluations to exchange rate |
| Privatization | In 1970 state owns 67 banks and firms; in 1973 state owns 251 and has intervened in 259 | In 1980 state owns 47 firms and one bank, including CODELCO | In 1990 state owns 41 firms and one bank, including CODELCO |
| Fiscal policy | "Cascade" sales/purchase tax; high public employment (12 percent of gainfully employed); high public deficits | VAT (20 percent); removal of wealth and profit taxes; indexation of taxes; public employment falls to 8 percent; public surplus (1979–81) | VAT down to 18 percent in 1990; public employment 6 percent; public surplus except 1986 |
| Internal credit | State control of interest rates; state-owned banks; credit controls | Free interest rate (1976–82); banks reprivatized; deregulation of capital markets; state bank not principal lender. | "Suggested" interest rate (1983–87); bank regulation, especially those in debt to central bank; capital markets regulated. |
| External debt | Capital controls; government main foreign debtor; control on foreign investment and private foreign debt | Free capital movement; private sector main foreign debtor; no discrimination against foreign investment; easy private credit | No private access to foreign loans; IMF and World Bank loans; debt renegotiation; no discrimination against foreign investment |

| | | | |
|---|---|---|---|
| Labor markets | High level of unionization; sectoral bargaining; close relation with political parties; public-sector unions influential; industrial tribunals and automatic wage adjustments | Repression of unions, no collective bargaining, and right to strike removed until 1979; indexed wages; new labor law (1979); more than one union per firm, collective negotiations at firm level only, voluntary affiliation, maximum sixty days strike, no industrial tribunals; emergency work programs: 500,000 in 1983; minimum wage abolished in 1979, reinstated in 1982 | Low level of unionization (11 percent); restricted biannual collective negotiation; public-sector unions banned; automatic wage adjustments ended; fall in minimum wage in relation to average wage; end of emergency work programs (1988) |
| Land market | More than half of farm land affected by agrarian reform; *latifundio* system eliminated | Progressive disposal of 10 million hectares in 3,700 properties held by state: 30 percent returned to original owners, 31 percent sold to new owners, 29 percent delivered to ex-tenants, 10 percent retained by state. *Latifundio* does not reappear; strong land market develops | Large tracts of nonagricultural land (most in forests) owned by state before 1970 sold or transferred to private interests; in agricultural sector, extensive subcontracting chains formed to link large exporters with medium and small producers |
| Social security | Contributions from both employers and employees with fiscal subsidy for the poorest third; nonwage costs high (40 percent of wages) | Reform 1981; private pension funds (AFPs) on individual contribution basis; nonactive workers financed by state during transition period | In 1991, 900,000 pensioners in old system; AFPs have 3.7 million members; nonwage costs low (3 percent of wages) |

SOURCES: P. Meller, "Revisión del proceso de ajuste chileno de la década del 80," *Colección Estudios CIEPLAN* no. 30 (Santiago, December 1990); and authors' analysis.

TABLE 2-3. *Integration into the World Economy, Selected Years, 1974–95*

| Indicator | 1974 | 1977 | 1980 | 1983 | 1986 | 1989 | 1992 | 1995 |
|---|---|---|---|---|---|---|---|---|
| Exports (billions of U.S. dollars) | 2.2 | 2.2 | 4.7 | 3.8 | 4.2 | 8.1 | 10.0 | 16.0 |
| Imports (billions of U.S. dollars) | 2.4 | 2.2 | 5.5 | 3.2 | 3.4 | 7.1 | 12.0 | 16.0 |
| Exports as percent of GDP | 20.4 | 20.6 | 22.8 | 24.0 | 30.6 | 32.0 | 35.9 | 37.3 |
| Number of exporters | 200 | 250 | 800 | 500 | 1,800 | 3,465 | 5,416 | 6,000 |
| Exports and imports as percent of GDP | 43.3 | 40.9 | 49.3 | 43.9 | 55.7 | 60.3 | 78.8 | 74.7 |
| Average nominal tariff (percent) | 75.0 | 22.0 | 10.0 | 18.0 | 20.0 | 15.0 | 11.0 | 11.0 |
| Index of nominal tariffs (1974 = 100) | 100.0 | 29.3 | 13.3 | 24.0 | 26.7 | 20.0 | 14.7 | 14.7 |
| Real exchange rate (1974 = 100) | 100.0 | 92.4 | 87.6 | 103.7 | 147.4 | 157.0 | 141.0 | 128.6 |
| Foreign debt (billions of U.S. dollars) | 4.0 | 5.3 | 10.9 | 17.2 | 20.0 | 16.3 | 18.2 | 21.3 |
| Foreign debt ratio to exports | 1.9 | 2.4 | 2.3 | 4.5 | 4.8 | 2.0 | 1.8 | 1.3 |

SOURCE: Central Bank of Chile.

policy led to a single exchange rate, the reduction and leveling off of tariffs to 10 percent (excluding cars), and the elimination of quotas. These were even enacted into constitutional law.

The result was a dramatic fall in protection for tradable and import-substituting goods. Within this framework, all prohibitions on imports were removed, and tariffs fell. This was not compensated for by a higher real exchange rate—given the massive increase in foreign loans but not foreign investment—which left the national economy extremely vulnerable. After the foreign debt crisis (1982–83), the government temporarily increased the degree of effective protection, opting for a form of structural adjustment that would allow the consolidation of an export model and trade surpluses. It was during this time that the "drawback" system was established, which favored the development of nontraditional exports.

Within a space of fifteen years, then, the Chilean economy was radically transformed through a unilateral process of opening to the exterior that was more pronounced in the commercial than the financial sector. During the 1980s, the growth rate of exports was nearly three times the growth rate of GDP; thus exports increased from 20.4 percent of GDP in 1974 to 32 percent in 1989. At the same time, the level of opening to the exterior rose from 43.3 percent to 60.3 percent (see table 2-3).

It is interesting to compare the cases of Chile and Mexico, which experienced similar processes of opening to the exterior but show considerable structural differences in terms of the importance of foreign trade and the degree of specialization of both economies. In 1990, exports and imports were 26 percent of GDP in Mexico, while in Chile they were over 68 percent. These are structural differences that emerge from the relative importance of the internal market. Another relevant factor is the degree of relative specialization in both economies. Mexico shows a more advanced level of industrialization and a greater dispersal of export goods, if gasoline and copper are excluded from the calculations.[1]

It should not be forgotten that the principal competitive advantage of Chilean exports was not so much low wages—as is the case with the *maquiladoras* in the majority of Latin American countries—but rather the country's vast quantities of renewable and nonrenewable natural resources, for which there is a high level of international demand. This has been the case particularly for mining, fishing, and forestry. For fruit exports, low wages have been important, although principally because they ensure very large profits for producers.

## Price Policy

One of the main transformations carried out by the state was the elimination of fixed prices negotiated with the private sector. Between 1973 and 1983, nearly 3,000 price controls were lifted—many at a time of hyperinflation and realignment of relative prices (1973–74)—although the military government retained control over strategic prices central to macroeconomic planning. The relative success of this stabilization policy (in terms of inflation control) opened the way for a monetarist policy, in which an attempt was made to develop an economic strategy based upon the monetary approach to the balance of payments. For a time markets were automatically coordinated through the use of the exchange rate as an anchor. Given the abundance of foreign credit, however, this policy led to massive foreign debt and the crisis of 1982–83.

This setback heralded a less orthodox form of neoliberalism. The structural adjustment of the 1980s was based on the realignment of relative prices to increase exports. Market coordination did not take place automatically, but through mini-devaluations in the exchange rate, "suggested" (in reality, controlled) interest rates, fixing of minimum wages so that their growth was always less than inflation, an agricultural pricing policy that favored the recovery of traditional agriculture, and an indexed tariff policy. This represented a form of indirect regulation of relative prices with three clear principles: raising the real exchange rate, increasing fiscal income, and reducing real wages.

## The Privatization of Public Firms

Although a wave of privatizations swept over most Latin American countries during the 1990s, this was not the case in Chile, where nearly all public companies had already been privatized between 1973 and 1990. Of the 25 banks, nearly 500 companies, and 3,700 farms under state control in 1973, only 41 firms (including CODELCO) and one bank were still in the hands of the government in 1990.[2]

Privatization in Chile took place in various stages and involved a number of different approaches. During the first phase (1973–74), firms that had been taken over under Popular Unity were returned to their original owners.[3] In the majority of cases, this occurred during the first months of the military government (during December 1973, around

260 firms were returned). At the same time, compensation was given to North American multinationals, especially to those affected by the expropriation of the copper and telecommunications industries. These payments amounted to $1.3 billion at 1988 prices.

The second stage (1975–82) was concurrent with liberalization of the financial system and of trade. CORFO, the state agency responsible for administering public firms, sold its share in 135 companies through auction.[4] This greatly strengthened certain national economic groups and led to a centralization of capital, which was considered necessary for the operation of the new economic model. Nevertheless, at the beginning of the 1980s state companies still had a substantial presence in the economy. Six out of the ten biggest companies in the country belonged to the state at the time.

The third stage (1983–85) represented a step back in the privatization program, as the external debt crisis led to the bankruptcy of economic groups that had taken control of most of the privatized banks and firms. The state intervened in the financial system and in an important number of large companies. But shortly afterward it began to re-privatize banks that had been restored to good health through the purchase of their liabilities by the Central Bank. In effect, this created a debt that would remain on the books over an indefinite time period.

The fourth stage (1985–89) affected two types of firms: those that had been the subject of state intervention during the external debt crisis and large public utilities. The procedures followed during the new privatizations were similar to those in other Latin American countries and allowed the participation of foreign capital, which began to invest as never before, taking advantage of the period of "popular capitalism"—a term that was in vogue at the time but has since gone out of fashion. Forms of privatization ranged from the classic system of bidding by business groups to the conversion of the external debt (debt-equity swaps), as well as the direct sale of shares to individuals.[5]

The fourth wave of privatization also included state firms that, until the middle of the 1980s, were efficient and generated surpluses for the state. Some of these companies (such as telephones and electricity) had been established between 1940 and 1950 with the aim of playing a fundamental role in national development. During the period from 1985 to 1990, and even after the plebiscite of October 1988, which Pinochet lost, some thirty companies were rapidly transferred to the private sector. These included leading companies in mining, steel, electricity, telecommunications, and food production. The state incurred great losses on the sales. It is estimated that, on average, they were sold for half their real value. Taking into account only the firms that were sold in 1986–87, one analyst calculated a loss of $600 million.[6] Despite the fact that privatization generated fiscal revenues, it also produced a sharp decline in state income. It has been estimated that between 1990 and 1997 the state will lose approximately $2.5 billion, which represents almost 8 percent of Chilean GDP.

## The Liberation and Expansion of Market Forces

The dismantling of trade barriers and controls, the privatization of firms, and increasing access to "macro-markets" between 1973 and 1990 led to a significant expansion of market forces in such fields as finance, labor, and land. New markets were also established in social security and health. The development of markets in areas where they either had not existed, or had been strongly controlled by natural monopolies or sectoral pressures (business, professional, or labor), led to a dismantling and reconstruction of many social networks and to the introduction of new forms of discipline on the actions of economic agents. It is important to note that this process developed more rapidly than the creation of rules or regulatory mechanisms, either formal or informal. Therefore, although the neoliberal reforms aimed to free up markets, deregulation produced chaotic situations because the state could not limit itself solely to a subsidiary role and was forced to make substantial interventions. Thus, although the power of private economic groups increased, the state retained its central role.

### *Liberalizing Capital Markets*

The development of financial markets and the reorganization of the banking system were the central elements of economic management in the 1980s. From 1974 on, the private financial sector developed very quickly in a context of abnormally high rates of interest. This culminated in the most profound crisis in the history of the Chilean banking system.

REORGANIZATION OF THE FINANCIAL SECTOR. Until 1973 the financial system had been made up of a number of small-scale private institutions, a very large state bank, and a savings and loans system (SINAP) that strictly belonged to neither the private nor the public sector. The scant importance of the financial sector can be seen in the fact that it represented only 4.5 percent of GDP in December 1970. The financial system was dominated by the public sector, which represented 31 percent of the total, followed by SINAP with a similar share, private corporations with 27 percent, and finally the private banking system with only 12 percent.

The process of change that was begun under the military regime demanded as a prior condition the reorganization of the financial sector in order to force the existing business sector—then financed, subsidized, and supported by the state—to become efficient, not through organized or administered capitalism, but through market mechanisms. The process of financial liberalization and centralization proceeded rapidly. As soon as the country had been brought under control in December 1973, interest rates were freed completely, removing all restrictions on private loans. Then in 1975, all banks under the authority of CORFO were auctioned off. Theoretically, there were legal limits on the ownership of banking assets, and the state was forbidden to invest in the sector. Nevertheless, these structures were unsuccessful in preventing participation in the privatization process by many companies belonging to the same owners. Faced with this situation, the government abolished legislation controlling the ownership of banks in 1978.

Once the market had been freed, new institutions emerged. In 1974 authorization was given for the formation of private financial organizations that could lend money to firms and individuals. In order to compete with the banks, these organizations captured funds at a higher interest rate and lent them at lower rates. This led to spectacular but ultimately insolvent growth, forcing the authorities to declare several institutions bankrupt.[7] At the end of 1976, the government found it necessary to call an abrupt halt to the experiment with unregulated banking and to increase sevenfold the minimum amount of capital needed to set up a financial institution.

During the early years of the military regime, guidelines covering foreign investment were also subject to dramatic changes. At the end of 1974, restrictions on foreign bank investment in Chile were lifted, and in January 1977 Chile formally withdrew from the Andean Pact, thus removing every obstacle to this type of investment.

As new forms of private banking emerged, the powers of the old financial system were reduced. In January 1978, for example, the monopoly formerly enjoyed by the Central Bank on financing productive activities through preferential loans was ended and the private banking system allowed to engage in similar activities. By this time as well, savings and loan associations, which formed an important part of the traditional financial sector, had been manipulated in a manner that quickly brought about their downfall. At the end of 1974, they were allowed to undertake new activities that included loans without interest rate restrictions. Then a few months later, in June 1975, the government restricted withdrawals from the savings accounts of associations to one a month. Given that the banks could undertake the same operations without restrictions, there was a massive fall in confidence among savings and loan customers and a severe crisis in the sector in September 1975. In one year, the twenty-one existing associations were reduced to one, and the latter disappeared completely in April 1980.

The weakening of the savings and loan system was accompanied by a parallel growth in the banking system.[8] Nevertheless, the large number of banks and financial societies did not lead to a subsequent fall in interest rates, which stood at six times the level of international rates, despite a period of excess liquidity. Growing financial difficulties eventually forced the Central Bank to "suggest" a system of interest rates, a practice that was not abandoned until December 1987.

EXCESSIVE DEBT AND THE 1982 CRISIS.    Spurred by faith in the self-regulation of the market, the military government removed all restrictions on foreign borrowing by banks at the end of 1979 and allowed private individuals or companies to receive loans in foreign currency as well. The obvious consequence was a further increase in foreign debt.[9] Most of this money was destined for consumption or for the purchase of firms, many of which were bankrupt; thus the accumulation of financial capital led to a massive growth in "paper companies," with very little productive investment.

The beginning of the decade saw an international recession that unleashed a financial crisis in Chile. In May 1981, one of the biggest private firms in the country (CRAV) collapsed under the weight of debt, dragging other firms and banks down with it. Interest rates increased still further, provoking a massive financial crisis. In December 1981, the superintendent of banking announced that financial institutions owed $2.5 billion—double the combined capital of all of them. The crisis dragged on through 1982, and the scale of the catastrophe was obvious by August of that year. Loans worth $1.236 billion had entered the country, with $1.148 billion leaving in the form of interest and amortizations. Twenty percent of the banks with foreign debt were in arrears.

From 1981 until 1984, emergency conditions prevailed. The Central Bank bought the overdue debt of the private banking system. By early 1982, national reserves had fallen by a billion dollars and the daily demand on the Central Bank by the banks was $22 million. The doubling of the price of the dollar in May 1982 led to a worsening of the debt crisis, forcing the government into a complete reversal of former policy. On January 13, 1983, three institutions (with a level of debt more than three times their assets) were liquidated. Another five (with debts of twice their net worth) were taken over, while two were kept under "observation." Within the following two years, fourteen out of twenty-six national banks and eight out of seventeen financial institutions came under state control. Paradoxically, the neoliberal government therefore came to exercise greater state control over the financial sector than had been the case during the government of Salvador Allende between 1970 and 1973.

The debt of these institutions was sold to the Central Bank. By the end of 1985 the deposits of banks and institutions that had been taken over by the state represented 98 percent of the deposits of the Central Bank and 30 percent of the deposits of the national banking system. These figures do not include funds that were written off. In a parallel process, negotiations took place for the repurchase of institutions that had been taken over by the Central Bank. Thus the private banking system was saved from bankruptcy by transferring its debts to the state.

Finally, the military regime abandoned its faith in the total deregulation of the financial system and initiated a period of strict control and vigilance. The new banking law, passed in 1986, placed limits on state guarantees for deposits at the same time that it gave wide powers of oversight to the superintendent of banks and finance. Such a policy reversal was required by the need to deal with the burgeoning public-sector debt. By 1988 the Central Bank owed more than $7 billion as a result of its salvage operation. Yet at the same time, ten banks owed the Central Bank $2.5 billion. Although there was no fixed repayment date—an irregular arrangement—this obliged the Treasury and Central Bank to coordinate policy and regulate the financial sector.

## The Labor Plan and the Deregulation of the Labor Market

After the violent repression of the first months and years of the military government, there was a lengthy period when the regulation of labor markets involved the exclusion of unions and collective bargaining. A new discipline was brought to bear upon the work force, based on repressive measures such as the dissolving of unions, as well as the elimination of index-linked wage increases, the end of state contributions to unions, and the prohibition of collective negotiations. This discipline was reinforced by a situation of high unemployment, in which the state intervened to cushion the effects of a low demand for labor through implementation of publicly funded emergency work programs.

In 1979 the period of "savage deregulation" gave way to one of legislated deregulation, as a new labor plan was introduced to replace the old labor code of 1931. The plan recognized the right to join a union, the right to collective negotiation, and the right to strike. Nevertheless, these rights were circumscribed by other regulations favorable to employers. Thus union affiliation was not compulsory (nor is it now), and employers had the authority to fire workers without giving cause. Within a company, there could be more than one union, with unaffiliated workers enjoying the results of concessions won by the unions. Although the right to strike was allowed, so was the right of employers to lock out workers or temporarily close the enterprise. The employer could contract temporary staff during a strike, and striking workers were not paid. Finally, after a certain number of days, workers had to return to work, accepting the last offer made or face dismissal. At the same time that the labor plan was introduced, the old industrial tribunals, which had tended to favor the workers, were dissolved. As finishing touches to the plan, central union organizations that had managed to survive were abolished in 1981 and some union leaders were expelled.

Union leaders did adapt to the new legislation, since it was preferable to the absolute deregulation that had existed until 1979. In comparison with the situation that had prevailed between 1973 and 1979, business leaders faced new restrictions, but these were more than offset by the flexibility with which they could use the labor force. The high rate of unemployment also allayed any fears they might have entertained. The number of unionized workers fell to below 10 percent of the work force, while the average size of unions was reduced by a third, and the number of unions with the right to negotiate fell by half. Not until 1988 did this situation begin to improve.

With the labor plan, labor market flexibility became a hallmark of business practice in the formal sector of the Chilean economy. Ending the system of collective contracts and developing a model of flexible individual contracts (with the exception of workers in the state copper industry and the Central Bank) increased the ability of the firm to impose changes in organization. This reduced functional differentiation, encouraged subcontracting, and increased temporary or fixed-term contracts. Reducing the capacity of unions to organize—whether through repression, the introduction of nonunionized labor relations, or increasing differentiation within the work force—gave employers much greater room for maneuver. Finally, the state policy of reducing the importance of the minimum wage allowed further erosion of any fixed component in wages while increasing the scope for variation in labor costs.

## Expansion of the Land Market

Until 1964 the predominant form of property in the Chilean countryside was the traditional large landholding, or estate, known as the *latifundio*.[10] Chilean agriculture during this period was oriented toward the internal market and depended upon state subsidies provided for the purpose of reducing the prices of food products with a low income elasticity of demand. Farm output was virtually stagnant for many years, and sectoral productivity declined during the 1950s at an annual rate of 0.4 percent. In consequence, Chile registered a trade deficit in agricultural products, and the sector fell further and further behind in relation to the rest of the economy.

Nevertheless, there were some signs of change in the agricultural sector from the 1940s on—related, among other factors, to the increasing fragmentation of large landholdings. Between 1955 and 1965, the number of agricultural holdings doubled, to reach 25,000. Attempts to modernize production were held back by the lack of genuine land markets as well as by old-fashioned management techniques.

At the end of the 1950s and the beginning of the 1960s, analyses suggested that the extreme concentration of property was one of the principal factors impeding agricultural development and limiting the contribution of this sector to the national economy. A consensus emerged that the responsibility for all national ills—real or imaginary—could be laid at the door of the *latifundio* and that it would be impossible to advance without increasing the supply of foodstuffs by bringing the peasantry into a closer relationship with the land and the market. In order to end the *latifundio* system and create efficient agriculture, agrarian reform was proposed.

The process began during the presidency of Eduardo Frei (1964–70) and gathered momentum under the Popular Unity government, with the support of an important peasant movement. Between 1964 and 1973, more than 5,000 holdings were expropriated, covering 10 million hectares, equivalent to 60 percent of the country's arable land.[11] It can be said without exaggeration that by 1973 there was not a single *latifundio* remaining in the country. Yet despite expectations, the military coup did not bring about a return of the *latifundio*. Instead, the authoritarian regime chose to give a new twist to the process, accelerating the privatization of agricultural property but also restructuring it and favoring the growth of a market economy in agriculture.

The first step was to return some of the expropriated land to its original owners: 30 percent of the 10 million hectares that had been expropriated was treated in this way. Another 10 percent was reserved for the state, and 31 percent was sold to new owners. The remaining 29 percent was given to ex-tenants.

In 1978 a law was passed that officially permitted the sale of land. Renting, land auctions, and the formation of private corporations thus became new possibilities. At a time when capital markets were undergoing liberalization, it was possible for "economic groups" to make different types of investment linked to agriculture. These ranged from export loans to commercial credit. Agriculture became more dynamic and more oriented toward the export sector, particularly fruit. It also grew more industrialized: "packings" and "tradings" became common expressions in the countryside. New firms and structures emerged, which, in the case of fruit production, represented 10,000 industrialized farms tied to trading companies that exported to markets in developed countries. And the value of Chilean agricultural exports rose from $21 million in 1973 to $683 million in 1988—a multiple of 33.

The export sector was concentrated overwhelmingly in the central valley, but there was also a sharp increase in productivity within traditional agriculture throughout the country. This led to the expansion of intermediate cities and new centers of regional development. Changes also took place in the forestry sector, where there was a new concentration of property. Together, these developments led to a boom in agriculture and forestry during the 1980s, favored by the increase in the real exchange rate, state subsidies, and a substantial imbalance in labor relations between owners and workers in the countryside.

## The Reform of the Social Security System

Among the most important of the modernizations undertaken by the authoritarian regime was the reform of social security in 1981. This transformed social security into a system of private savings administered by private capital.

Since 1924 Chile had developed a system of social security with wide coverage for old age, incapacity, and death, as was the case for similar programs in Europe. The majority of the urban population belonged to one of three schemes: the social security system, the public employees' fund, or the fund for private workers. The state was completely responsible for administering these welfare funds.

By 1981 there was a strong consensus that the system was in a disastrous condition. It was based upon over 2,000 general laws and 3,000 complementary laws. There were thirty social security offices and seventy welfare services, as well as numerous complementary organizations, and complaints regarding maladministration were widespread. Over and above administrative problems, however, there was a clear economic problem. Resources devoted to social security (including family allowances, pensions, and other forms of social support) grew from almost 20 percent of fiscal expenditure in 1973 to 50 percent in 1980.

It is interesting to note that the reform of the system did not originate in the Finance or Economic Ministries, but rather in the Ministry of Labor, which was run at the time by José Piñera, a Harvard-trained economist. The arrangement proposed by Piñera and his associates was simple: there would be no shared responsibilities or state administration. Instead, each employee would be obliged to save a significant part of his or her income—not less than 10 percent—and hand it over to a private entity that would be responsible for investing it. These entities, which were to become known as AFPs (pension administration funds), were required to guarantee with their own assets the moneys deposited with them. This gave workers a certain degree of security when choosing an AFP. The system permitted members to switch their savings from one AFP to another, but their level of personal savings was the only factor determining final benefits.

At the same time, the creation of the AFPs had the important effect of permitting the formation, practically overnight, of a new business class that did not need large amounts of its own capital in order to establish itself. All the capital the new *empresarios* needed came from the members of the AFPs themselves.

The state assigned itself a minimal role in regulating the operation of the system, and it guaranteed a minimum pension for workers who could not finance the most basic contributions during their working life. Workers were expressly forbidden from participating in the new form of administration. There was absolutely no tendency toward joint management or any other kind of vaguely socializing formula, such as cooperatives. Pension funds were centralized in private hands; it was assumed that this would be the best guarantee for the worker.

Curiously, workers switched pension systems with surprising ease. Within a year, almost 30 percent of them had made the change. It is not clear whether this was due to the excellence of the system or because, in the depressed world of incomes and pensions in 1980, the state had promised a 10 percent wage increase for those who made the change. At any rate, the reforms of 1981 brought about an accelerated liberalization of the pension system. The old savings funds were prevented from taking on new members, and only those who had already reached old age were permitted to remain within the earlier programs.

A year and a half later, economic crisis forced the state to take over the AFPs. Shortly afterward, however, they were put up for sale, and some mergers took place. This in turn allowed the entrance of foreign capital. Thus of the fourteen AFPs in Chile, more than half are controlled by foreign consortia. At the same time, two AFPs control more than 60 percent of the total accumulated capital.

The reform of the social security system allowed the massive resources created by active workers to be channeled toward the private sector. It was purely and simply a case of liberating funds for capitalist accumulation. Nevertheless, the weaknesses of the financial system were such that the activities of the AFPs had to be closely regulated. These regulations, designed in times of crisis, seriously limited the range of investment possibilities for pension funds, which could be used only for low-risk projects, such as large enterprises with a solid history of earnings. This led to a progressive accumulation of funds that could not be converted into productive saving or investment.

Only in 1992 did parliament debate a project to reform the capital markets, devoting particular attention to the AFPs. The result was a new law that broadened investment opportunities, while also limiting the exercise of monopoly control and improving the likelihood that contributors would be informed of their investments and of the administrative charges involved.

### Fiscal Adjustment and Social Services

Finally, during the first decade of the military regime, a profound fiscal adjustment took place, dedicated to reducing the importance of tariffs as a source of fiscal income, increasing the efficiency of indirect taxation, and reducing spending. In the case of social policy, this reduction was to be balanced by increased targeting of resources toward the poorest sectors.

Since Chile had an extensive foreign debt, reducing the fiscal deficit was essential and demonstrated the capacity of the state to gain autonomy from the pressures of different social sectors. At the same time, normalizing the finances of the Central Bank was also a key indication of the capacity of the government to confront the constant imbalances of a peripheral or semiperipheral economy.

This led to a break with the old pattern of growth in the provision of social services. Over a number of decades before 1973, services such as health, social security, telecommunications, and infrastructure had been run by the state and were oriented toward satisfying the demand of high- and middle-income groups before being extended to poorer sectors. In fact, much of the legitimacy of the state was derived in this way. A fast expansion of public services led to a growing level of fiscal deficit. It also led to the increasing immobility of large quantities of financial capital.

The reforms that took place in Chile created a new form of legitimation very different from the old bureaucratic populist model. The privatization of significant areas within the public health and education programs, involving open or implicit subsidies for those choosing to satisfy these needs through the market, allowed high- and middle-income groups access to services of better quality than those operated by the public sector. At the same time, the reduction of social spending and increased targeting toward specific projects (such as the reduction of infant mortality) led to an overall deterioration in access to public services for low-income groups. Partial privatization in health and education also freed up surpluses that were trapped in the public sector and converted them into private capital.

## The Myth of the "Subsidiary" State

There is a false, albeit widely accepted, idea that neoliberalism in Chile involved a state that intervened in a "subsidiary" fashion only when private enterprise was not effective, and that markets were left to function freely or savagely (depending on one's viewpoint) without the interference of the state. The idea that the neoliberal state worked only to liberate markets, while withdrawing progressively from the economy, takes no account of the real role of the state in Chile between

1973 and 1990. On the contrary, the state was highly interventionist, and five basic arguments support this contention.

First, traditional indicators of the level of public spending (excluding public debt repayments and fiscal revenue) as a percentage of GDP were higher under the military regime than in 1961–70. During 1983–88, average government spending as a proportion of GDP was 25.1 percent, while in 1967–72 it was 23.6 percent. Between 1983 and 1988, average tax income as a proportion of GDP was 25.6 percent, compared with 21.2 percent between 1967 and 1972. Fiscal revenues were indexed so that they would not erode with inflation.

Second, although the public sector was larger in 1973 than it is at present, state agencies were subject to multiple social and political pressures that prevented them from acting in a coherent manner. This was a major problem for both the Frei and Allende governments. After 1973 the reverse was true: the state was almost totally protected from social pressure, and the power of the executive was virtually unlimited. As the state has grown more compact, its structure has also become more hierarchical, which has increased its capacity for intervention in society and the economy.

Third, it should not be forgotten that it was public ownership of the copper industry, nationalized during the Allende government, that gave the military government important fiscal revenues, preventing it from having to demand more from the rest of the economy. It has been estimated that the nationalization of copper alone provided the state with additional resources of more than U.S. $10 billion between 1974 and 1989,[12] which had a very positive effect on the balance of payments and fiscal accounts.

Fourth, in spite of the fact that the range of products and activities under price control was dramatically reduced from 1973 on, the state maintained strategic control over relative prices. Through systematic changes to the exchange rate, interest rates, public tariffs, and agricultural prices, the state took an active role in determining the level of prices and profits in the economy. No less significant were coercive state regulations of labor markets and wages. Through the simple mechanism of restricting union activity and collective negotiations, wages were held down, especially for large numbers of people engaged in precarious employment.[13]

Finally, it is important to note that during the period between 1985 and 1988, half the income of extremely poor groups in Chile came from subsidies and fiscal support. All of these indicators bear witness to the fiscal and monetary importance of the state and—after the crisis of 1981–83—to increasing state regulation of the economy in ways that were never neutral but were intended to promote specific kinds of behavior on the part of economic agents.

In fact, during the 1980s, in the middle of structural adjustment toward an export-based economy, the neoliberal state—far from being reduced to a subsidiary role—actually strengthened its position in the Chilean economy. Taking a historical perspective, it is clear that, given a deepening crisis and growing resistance from civil society at this time, the realization of the free-market utopia required an extensive strengthening of the state.

Government attempts to liberalize markets suffered serious setbacks due to market failures, and there were thus objective limits to further deregulation. For one thing, there was a series of public goods and services that could only partially be provided by markets alone, such as health, education, and the environment. This meant that the sphere of action of the state had to remain considerably wider than that envisaged by neoliberal doctrine. Second, given that the immense majority of markets did not conform to the idealized neoclassical model, the need for regulation of privatized industries quickly became apparent. This was especially the case for natural monopolies and markets with profound information imbalances. The banking industry and telephone and electric companies were good examples of this. Further problems requiring state intervention, including unfair competition and disorganized markets, emerged with the opening to the exterior.

Attempts at regulation, which began to be implemented during the 1980s, faced fairly serious obstacles. These included the weakness of some state institutions when dealing with powerful economic groups, the absence of adequate information systems, and strong pressure from technocrats who, in their conversion into economic groups, had taken with them an extensive knowledge of the functioning of the state. Nevertheless, there continued to be an inexorable tendency toward the construction of new forms of regulation during the 1980s. Paradoxically, the radical nature of the neoliberal subsidiary state required an increase in public intervention.

## Institutional Transformations

Thus we conclude, first, that the free-market reforms could be implemented only because of the existence of a strong state; and second, that the consequences of these reforms did not include a weakening of the state. Although the state retired from some functions (such as public-sector companies), it was strengthened in others (macroeconomic policy). But the study of institutional changes occurring within Chilean capitalism should not focus exclusively on what occurred in the sphere of state and markets. The fundamental changes taking place between 1973 and 1990 involved not only the public sector and markets but also private-sector institutions, such as economic groups and firms, as well as mechanisms of coordination other than those of markets.

During this period, economic institutions, like social structures, were subject to simultaneous processes of dismantling and restructuring. This progress was sometimes concealed behind more visible transformations such as deregulation and privatization, which can create a distorted—if convenient—view of what was actually taking place at the time. After all, the general discussion of a transition from state-dominated to free-market economy—without looking too much further into specific cases—provides a common consensus between left and right, although they might disagree as to whether the consequences of the transition have been positive or negative.

Part of this consensus rests on descriptions of the expansion of decentralized markets governed by price mechanisms and the concomitant weakening of old command hierarchies. Nevertheless, coordination among private economic agents does not take place in idealized markets, without subjects and power relations, but in unequal markets that are influenced by public regulations and economic groups. There are also many kinds of transactions, involving both formal and informal contracts, that go beyond the limits of the market.[14]

In Chile, as in every capitalist country, coordination among economic agents takes place not only through markets but also through mechanisms of hierarchy and command. In the private sphere, such command takes place within the firm.[15] Hierarchies among economic agents appear within conglomerates, such as the private economic groups that have developed so spectacularly during the past few decades in Chile. New types of formal and informal subcontracting, in which larger firms impose conditions on an unequal basis, are now very common. It is no exaggeration to say that the growth of powerful conglomerates and the extension of their control over smaller firms has been as important a development in recent Chilean economic history as the opening toward international markets.

It would appear something of a paradox that in an economy increasingly open to the world market, internal hierarchical organizations were strengthened rather than weakened. But the vast majority of markets are based on firms or groups that depend for their competitive edge on their power and organizational efficiency. This has been clearly seen in various Asian countries with a strong link between the state and economic groups and in the United States with the close link between corporations and the public sector (for example, the military-industrial complex).

## The Reorganization of Capital: Economic Groups

Practically all sectors of the Chilean economy are currently controlled by large firms that in turn belong to economic groups. More than at any other stage in its history, Chile is dominated by conglomerates—national or foreign—that were strengthened by the economic policies carried out between 1973 and 1990. The dictatorial state not only saved them financially but also sold them efficient state companies at undervalued prices, and then resold the companies of the economic groups that went bankrupt in the 1981–83 crisis.

The new economic groups are no longer based primarily on "paper" companies, but now are composed of firms with "chimneys": in other words, they link financial and productive sectors. Diversification in investment appears to be the golden rule of the principal groups, and they always try to gain control over market leaders, thus obtaining monopoly profits.

The conglomerates have gone through a learning process that has allowed them to develop in a different way than in the past. First, they are more professional than before; and, even when they remain in the hands of families, younger generations are given postgraduate training. Second, ownership is more indirect. This is not only for tax purposes but also to free up capital. The tendency is to centralize ownership in investment societies. Third, they are more diversified and governed by a professional logic that facilitates forward planning. The fundamental objective is to maximize the rate of expansion in order to raise the average profit rate. Fourth, toward the end of the 1980s the economic groups became more internationalized, forming alliances with foreign conglomerates and making direct investments in Latin America and financial investments in developed countries. Fifth, the national groups are "price takers" at the international level and "price makers" at the national level.

The economic groups are the principal source of independent decisionmaking within the Chilean economy. Not only do they make decisions with regard to prices and output; they also decide the level, time span, and location of investment and how such investments are financed. These decisions are of fundamental importance for the national economy. It is therefore worth reiterating that throughout the period from 1973 to 1990, the state favored the growth of these national economic conglomerates, which have perfected their internal organization and gained not only business experience but also increasing autonomy from the state. They have also established direct links with the international financial system.

### The Transformation of the Firm

What actually takes place within the factory or company walls often tends to be overlooked. Yet it is in the microcosm of production that many of the important secrets of this capitalist recovery are ultimately to be found.

RATIONALIZATION, 1973–83.   Between 1973 and 1979 the way was cleared for transformation of enterprises through repression of the union movement, enactment of new labor legislation, and the firing of the most combative sectors of the working class. Particularly from 1975 on, there was a process of intense capitalist rationalization associated with the removal of obstacles to foreign trade. The crisis of 1981–83 was the catalyst that led firms to streamline dramatically; whole divisions were removed, workers sacked, and surplus or obsolete machinery scrapped.

One of the most striking aspects of this process was the reduction in vertical integration within firms. Many of them not only got rid of entire sections but also began a systematic policy of subcontracting parts of the production process that they had previously carried out themselves. For technical reasons this was less pronounced in industries with continuous or semicontinuous production processes. But in general the economic groups promoted a formal legal dismantling of large companies, creating specialized subsidiaries with a degree of financial autonomy. This has continued until today, not only in response to the need to rationalize production processes still further but also to enhance the mobility of financial capital.

At the workplace level, the principal change involved the increasingly intensive use of Taylorist methods of organization and control, which could not be fully used in the previous period.[16] During the 1960s, many owners attempted with little success to rationalize their industrial plant, but there were three main obstacles. First, the scale of production was greater than the size of the markets, leading to the need for a mixture of diverse products with different production techniques. This had the effect of intensifying production line problems. Second, labor legislation and the strength of the unions produced continuous resistance to rationalization plans. Third, businesses were often incapable of adequately incorporating new forms of management and organization. Therefore they alternated between compromise with the work force and attempts at rationalization. When these attempts failed, businesses would demand compensation from the state.

Nevertheless, during the first decade of authoritarian rule, all the obstacles to rationalization were overcome. In the face of external competition, and with an authoritarian state that was always prepared to use an iron hand in enforcing repressive labor legislation, employers were able to break the unions, do away with the model of collective contracts, and dramatically alter the incentive system. The result was not only a fall in wages but an increase in control over the work force and above all the increased flexibility in the use of labor.

The owners achieved three types of flexibility. The first was functional flexibility, with the capacity to relocate workers in different functions or departments within the firm and none of the legal obstacles or resistance by unions that had marked the period before 1973. The second was labor flexibility, with the capacity to hire or fire with very little legal restriction. The third was the capacity to reduce wages in crisis situations with no effective resistance, given that the rate of unionization did not exceed 12 percent.

The method was repressive and always accompanied by systematic attempts to curb union power. It was further aided by draconian labor legislation. Hence the dictatorial state was associated with widespread authoritarian practices within the firm. This authoritarian rationalization was imposed under a one-sided logic; worker resistance against the economic model was important at the national level, but it came from outside the factory rather than within it. Workers simply did not have the capacity to organize large strikes. The freedom of action for owners and managers of enterprises was thus very high; they could organize production as suited them best, and the only restriction on the speed and intensity of change was the capacity of the firm itself. This explains why, by the middle of the 1980s, the Chilean production system was capable of a sustained recovery based on low wages, heavy work schedules, flexible use of the labor force, aggressive commercial strategies, and a competitive advantage in mining and agriculture.

AUTHORITARIAN TECHNOLOGICAL MODERNIZATION. Although technological and organizational change characterized the period from 1983 to 1989, this situation contained an important paradox. A great deal of evidence points to the fact that modern technologies were combined with Taylorist work practices dating from the beginning of the century. The novelty in Chile was therefore nothing more than flexibility in the use of labor, in conditions that did nothing to improve the employment conditions of the work force. This strange combination of the new and the old was the basis of what has been called the neo-Taylorist road to modernization.[17]

The social consequences of such a form of modernization have been and continue to be extremely unsatisfactory for the country. On the one hand, there is a body of workers with stable jobs, relatively high wages, and multifaceted, creative tasks. Without constituting a new "labor aristocracy," this is a minority group. On the other hand, there is a great mass of workers with highly precarious employment conditions. This includes not only temporary workers in the countryside but hundreds of thousands of subcontracted workers who do not have fixed contracts or the ability to join a union, much less the option of collective negotiation. They carry out monotonous tasks, with no possibility of participating in the management of the firm.

Furthermore, in banks and service companies where conditions are supposedly better for nonprofessional workers, another paradox is apparent. The very rapid introduction of new information technologies is converting the office of the future into the factory of the past, in a way reminiscent of Garson's concept of the "electronic sweatshop."[18] Workers engage in repetitive operations, leading to exhaustion and nervous disorders. This harsh use of the labor force and the worsening of capital-labor relations is a reflection of the methods favored by neo-Taylorism.

## Establishing Production Chains

Increasing flexibility and efficiency within the Chilean production system is explained not only by what took place inside the firm, but also by the establishment of subcontracting chains linking large firms with small and medium ones, many characterized by low productivity. Such chains exist in fruit production, fishing, and forestry, and they are being developed in mining and the garment industry. Telecommunications perform a fundamental role in this process.

There is a very unequal power relation in these production chains, which are dominated by oligopolies belonging in turn to economic groups. The subcontracted firms operate almost as departments of a big firm, although they are independent of it. Within this system, there is a certain amount of competition among oligopolies and an extremely high degree of competition among the subcontractors.

The small and medium firms that form part of production chains are of two types: either they are relatively new companies whose owners are professionals or tradespeople of urban origin, or they are older firms that have been reconverted. Some (fruit) have incorporated more technology and capital, and others (fishing, wood) less, but all have modernized in order to become part of these production chains. The workers of such companies are nonunionized, the majority work for low wages, and they perform specialized tasks. The use of Taylorist methods is much less prevalent than in the larger firm, but certain techniques are imposed from outside. The forms of specialization required by the production chain and, in many cases, the kind of technical advice offered by the oligopolistic firms (as in the case of fruit production) tend to reproduce Taylorist practices.

The extensive use of subcontracting allows large firms to shift costs and risks to smaller enterprises, while surpluses are transferred from the subcontracted firm (and its work force) to the economic group that dominates the network. Obviously it is difficult for subcontracted firms to grow into larger, more modern companies when they must have such a short-term horizon, they bear most of the brunt of changes in the economic cycle, there is no adequate state regulation of their relations with contractors, and the state permits them to transfer all of their costs to the work force.

## The Concentration of Power and Income

In sum, there has been an immense transfer of surpluses, operating in four key directions:

—From the state to large capital. This took place first between 1982 and 1983, when the state used public funds to solve the crisis in the financial sector, and again between 1985 and 1989, when thirty efficient profit-making public firms were sold at knockdown prices.

—From wages to profits, or from the poor to the rich. This is epitomized in the fall of average real and minimum wages. This was not simply a case of wages failing to keep up with inflation. As an outcome of a specific government attack on the minimum wage, workers also had to work for far lower wages than had been the case in the past. The process of expropriation of the incomes of the poor—who are mostly workers—was so intense that by 1988 the share of national income of the richest 10 percent of the population had risen to almost 42 percent. Ten years earlier it had been 35 percent.

—The transfer of income toward the export sector. This was possible because between 1983 and 1989 the real exchange rate rose much faster than other prices in the economy (in other words, the peso remained relatively undervalued). Such a change in relative prices signified a massive transfer of resources from society in general to the export sector, dominated by the big economic conglomerates.

—The increasing rate of destruction of natural resources. The cost of this form of deterioration does not show up either in firms' balance sheets or in the national accounts. There is a close relationship between the exploitation of the labor force and the destruction of natural resources, representing the "transfer" of surplus extracted from the national heritage to private economic groups.

# 3

# The Actors:
# From Classes to Elites

Who were the principal actors in this process of structural adjustment that had such an impact upon Chilean society? What was the role played by the military, the technical teams, and the business sector?

As mentioned above, political transformation—the move from dictatorship to democracy—was principally the work of an opposition to the military regime that broke away from a heterogeneous and disruptive social movement and managed to insert itself into the authoritarian political institutions. This led to a revival of the civilian political class and the renovation of the old party system. The identification of the actors involved in the process of economic transformation would appear to be more straightforward, but is not as clear as it seems at first sight.

Two different approaches are often used to answer this question. The first, of a structural nature, consists of identifying the social groups who benefited most from the economic transformations and attributing to them responsibility in the last instance for the corresponding decisions. The second approach involves constructing the framework of relations within which the principal decisions were made, placing in it the subjects who intervened in these decisions, identifying the procedure and consistency of the state elite, and reconstructing their relations with social groups from different situations at critical moments.

Following the first of these approaches, the answer is fairly brief. In the short and medium term, those most favored by the economic transformations that took place under the military regime can be identified as the small number of conglomerates or economic groups that came to control, in a few years, the principal financial, industrial, and commercial institutions of the country. But in sociology, as in criminal investigation, it is not enough to establish who benefits from an event in order to determine its author. And, in the case of Chile, the specific influence of the business sector, including the powerful economic groups, was considerably less direct than is often thought. An examination of the actual history of these transformations suggests that the mediation of an elite with autonomy from the immediate interests of distinct factions or economic power groups was fundamental in bringing these changes about.

## The Business *Gremios*

The identification of the business sector as the decisive actor in the economic transformation (sometimes claimed by this sector itself), stems from a confusion between the origins of the military government and the origins of the economic policy that it carried out. However, they need to be carefully separated, as this distinction changed the character of the government from simply reactive to foundational or revolutionary.

The Chilean business class played a decisive role in the opposition to the socialist government of Salvador Allende and Popular Unity, as well as in its destabilization and overthrow. During that time, business organizations moved directly from sectoral pressure to political struggle and were notably successful in maintaining the discipline of their affiliates, particularly when it came to calls for the most radical forms of mobilization.

The older sectoral organizations of big business had preserved for some time their role as economic pressure groups without transferring their activities to the political field. (These included many with a long history, such as the National Agricultural Society, founded in 1838; the Central Confederation of Commerce, founded in 1858; the National Mining Society and the National Industrial Society, both founded in 1883; and more recent additions such as the Association of Banks and Financial Institutions, created in 1943; or the Chilean Construction Chamber, founded in 1951.) Nevertheless, they came together, even before the Popular Unity government, in the Confederation of Production and Commerce, with the aim of defending the role of business in society and the right to private property. They were concerned about the "socializing threat" that had been initiated by the agrarian reform, which they felt to be embodied in the principal political forces of the country (the Communist and Socialist parties on the left, as well as the Christian Democrats).

Within the context of a political right whose fortunes were in decline, the creation of the confederation at the end of the 1960s signified an attempt to unite the owners of businesses as a social class, over and above their specific corporate interests, and to incorporate medium and small firms. The numerical force of these sectors, as will be shown later, would be decisive in first resisting policies of state expropriation and later moving to a quasi-insurrectional position.

But such attempts had not been completely successful in the past. For several decades big business organizations had encountered difficulties in uniting small businesses around them. The latter were organized principally in the Confederation of Retail Traders and Small Industry (founded in 1938) and the transport federations (the Chilean Truck Owners Federation and the National Federation of Independent Taxis, both founded in 1953; the National Federation of Chilean Bus Owners, founded in 1958; and smaller organizations). These organizations had maintained a degree of independence from, and also entered habitually into conflict with, the organizations of big business. They were dependent upon the evolution of an internal market, were motivated by a middle-class discourse, and made protectionist demands on the state (against external competition as well as against monopolistic control of internal markets). Their leaders had historically maintained close links with centrist or national-populist political currents and they vigorously asserted their difference from the big bosses (whom they pejoratively referred to as the "economic right").

The period of Popular Unity offered the opportunity to overcome these historic differences and replace them with the logic of a proprietary class defending corporate interests. In the government program of the forces of the left, proposals for expropriation were limited to large agricultural property and the large financial, industrial, and distributive monopolies. This was precisely because the left recognized diversity in the behavior of the different leaders of the business sector. However, the popular base that constituted the government's support quickly demanded more expropriation than that contained in the government program.

As has already been mentioned, the class base of radical unionism could be found much more in small and medium businesses than in the large enterprises. The "antimonopolistic" reforms of Popular Unity, which sought the alliance or at least the neutrality of the middle sectors, did not provide immediate solutions for the workers of such firms. Yet it was in these firms, precisely because of their economic weakness and the high significance of wages in their cost structures, that worker-owner conflict over wages and conditions was especially acute. The lack of immediate government policy toward these firms created a gap that would be filled by direct pressure from the masses themselves.

Limited to carrying out its reforms within the framework of existing legality, and in the absence of adequate legislation to nationalize firms through expropriation, the Allende government resorted to two parallel mechanisms for the formation of the social area of the economy that had been set out in its program. On the one hand, it negotiated the purchase of important share packages for the state. On the other, it "intervened" in companies (through the replacement of management with a government-designated administrator) on the grounds of mal-administration.[1] Motivated by the fact that they could count on a sympathetic government, many unions from small and medium companies began indefinite strikes over wages. This was done in the knowledge that if they did not achieve their demands, the government would be obliged to intervene in the company—as effectively happened in the majority of cases—and replace the owners with designated administrators.

This process, which expanded the original program of expropriation, was rapidly accompanied by other forms of action from below. These were principally indefinite occupations of urban lands or agricultural sites that were not legally subject to expropriation, as a means of applying pressure on the government to bring about their expropriation. Increasingly, therefore, the assurances given by the leadership of Popular Unity to small and medium companies that their properties would not be affected by the expropriation policies of the Allende government disappeared into thin air.

In contrast to the forecasts of the left, the conflict between the Allende government and small and medium firms was more acute than the confrontation between the government and big business. While the small and medium firms were soon engaged in a pitched battle against the unions and the practice of intervention, the large companies acted within a market logic, negotiating directly with the Ministry of the Economy to secure acceptable prices for the sale of packages of shares in their companies to the state. For this reason, it was the small and medium firms, rather than their larger counterparts, who were the first to move directly to radical political struggle against the Allende government.

With all of this, by the end of 1971 the organizations of diverse strata and factions of the business class converged to form a solid movement in the defense of private property. The organizations of big business took on the radical discourse of the small and medium firms in the face of what they saw as the threatened disappearance of the private sector. As Guillermo Campero writes, the first common mobilization took place around an issue loaded with symbolic meaning: "opposition to the government purchase of shares in the Paper and Cardboard Manufacturing Company. Presiding over this semi-monopolistic company was the ex-President and ex-candidate for the Presidency of the Republic in 1970, Jorge Alessandri. It was a central and symbolic nucleus of Chilean capitalism."[2]

What followed this unification of the business associations and their adoption of political struggle is well known. These organizations, acting jointly with other representative bodies of the middle sectors (principally professional organizations and some staff organizations from the copper industry), unleashed an aggressive mobilization that reached its highest point in October 1972 and August 1973 with the great "employers' strikes." These disrupted national production and distribution for prolonged periods and provided the context for those plotting the military coup that would overthrow the constitutional government.

The radical mobilization of the *gremios* (such was the name by which these diverse organizations established a common identity) had two political effects of the utmost importance. First, as was shown in chapter 1, it supplanted political parties as the leading force of the opposition and, in particular, left the centrist parties little scope for maneuver. Secondly, it precipitated the conversion of the military command, which Allende had brought into government to combat the strikes and fill the gap left by the parties of the center, into a major political actor. The direct negotiations that the military and *gremio* leaders carried out during the Allende administration would form an important precedent for the creation of the power bloc that emerged with the coup d'état in 1973.

Neither these facts, nor the strong allegiance quickly pledged by the majority of *gremio* leaders to the military government, explains the adoption of the neoliberal model by the Pinochet government within a short space of time. As Campero correctly states, "The coalition of the various *gremio* sectors came about through the articulation of a common principle of opposition and not because they had developed a united socio-economic project for the future."[3]

Campero gives two principal reasons why this did not occur: In the first place, business organizations lacked a persistent practice of reflection on the social order and alternatives for change. "Many *gremios* of big or small firms tended to consider themselves more as subjects of the established order than agents of social transformation. As a result, their perspective was less defined by 'socio-political projects' than by a logic of adaptive economic behavior and/or of competition."[4]

In the second place, the very "heterogeneity of strictly economic interests militated against common projects, since the relations of domination between big and medium or small business were evident."[5] What held these groups together was a common fear of a socialist threat to property, but they had no coherent vision of an alternative society. This would become clear during the first months of military government with the reappearance of important differences between distinct *gremios* and with the difficulties experienced by the military government in defining, over and above emergency anti-inflationary measures, a coherent model of political economy.

Campero documents the various perspectives that emerged by the second day of military government on how to preserve the power of the *gremios* in the new circumstances. The *gremios* of small and medium firms, under the leadership of the Truckers' president, León Vilarín, insisted on maintaining the *gremios* as a movement "both of dialogue with and mobilized support for the government."[6] However, the big firms (led at the time by the president of the Confederation of Production and Commerce, Jorge Fontaine) maintained that "the *gremios* should further the goal of national unity, promoting development, social justice and the restoration of moral values. It would therefore be a great mistake to become a big political party or a substitute for one. We are men of work and what interests us is production."

Nor was there agreement, whether among the *gremios* or within the government, with respect to economic policy. Tomás Moulián and Pilar Vergara have shown how, within the government, no group enjoyed a clear hegemony among the technocrats and civilian economists who had been called upon to collaborate in "national reconstruction."[7] Consensus was limited to a general framework of common principles (private property, free competition, opening to international trade) and a body of urgent measures to meet the needs of the moment (devaluation, freeing prices, a restrictive wage policy, fiscal moderation, the return of expropriated and "intervened" firms, indemnities for foreign companies that had been nationalized under the previous government). But in relation to economic strategy, there was neither clarity nor consensus.

## A Civilian Technocracy: The "Chicago Boys"

Agreement on the need to react to a common threat, without an accepted common project for the future, led to a growing concentration of power, not only within the military high command, but also within a newly created civilian technocracy, formally independent from the distinct business factions. The bonds of loyalty that were established between this technocratic group and General Pinochet permitted the development of a military dictatorship that was not simply reactionary but would also instigate a capitalist revolution.

The best study of this technocratic elite, by Juan Gabriel Valdés, argues on the basis of a wide range of interviews that

> the admirals and generals who took power in Chile in 1973 did not have a defined project for government. The doctrine of National Security to which they made constant reference ... could not produce the design for an efficient relationship between the state and civil society. The Chilean Armed Forces lacked experience in government and were forced into action, not with a determined plan to impose a military administration, but rather as a reaction against what they considered to be a grave threat to national security and their very institutional existence: the Allende administration and the radicalization of the political and social situation.
>
> This deficiency made itself particularly apparent in the economic sphere. The Navy, which initially took charge of the economy, agreed only on the gravity of the situation. ... Nevertheless, the new authorities lacked technical training in economic matters. Clearly, this does not mean that they did not have a general ideological position. Owing to their background in the middle or upper classes, as well as their conservative traditions, the officers of the Chilean Navy instinctively favored liberal economic policies and detested the socialist project of Popular Unity.
>
> From the end of 1972, some high naval officers had made contact with a group of opposition economists who were secretly working on an alternative plan for government. The plan was ready for the

day of the military coup and had been distributed to the officials of the three branches of the Armed Forces who initially occupied positions in the government. The new authorities, however, motivated probably by a desire for international recognition in this field, opted at first for those people they considered to have the greatest prestige.[8]

Among those with whom contact was made, according to the information offered by Valdés, were important figures linked to the Christian Democrat government of Eduardo Frei: ex-ministers Sergio Molina and Raúl Sáez as well as the ex-president of the Central Bank, Carlos Massad. Sáez, an engineer associated with the structuralist economic school developed during the 1960s by the Economic Commission for Latin America (CEPAL), enjoyed great international prestige. He effectively became the minister for finance and economics under the military regime, which confirms, without a doubt, that the influence of the neoliberal economic team was not as great at the time as some have later claimed.

Economic concepts that enjoyed currency, at least during the first year of military rule, appear to have had more to do with a political than a strictly technical logic. In effect, the central point that was being debated during the early definition of an economic strategy was the very character of the military government. A strategy of "restoration," or return to the old equilibrium that had been broken during the Popular Unity period, implied at the same time a definition of the military government as a parenthesis between two civil administrations—a period of repressive pacification after which power would be returned to the party with the greatest electoral strength and parliamentary representation (the Christian Democrat party).[9]

The logic of centralizing power in the president of the military junta, which corresponded to a "Portalist" ideology within the armed forces, was, however, incompatible with this scenario.[10] Neither the aspirations of the Christian Democrat party (for which the Army High Command still reserved a strong resentment, owing to the scant attention the Frei government had paid to their desire for institutional modernization), nor those of the *gremios,* who tried to set up a corporatist model of political participation, came close to being realized. The legitimation (by the military junta and its president) of a total replacement of the traditional party system, and even of the social base that had supported the coup, had to be based on a different order from that which had existed before the Popular Unity government. There were no ready-made groups to form the basis for this new order, which would require a long period of control by a "tutor." The simple idea of normalization of the economy had to be replaced by the creation of a new economic order. Clearly the radical project of the neoliberal economists, who would later become known as the "Chicago Boys,"[11] was far more congruent with such ideas than the pragmatic realism of the other civil advisors to the military junta. On this point, they enjoyed a decisive comparative advantage.

But who were these neoliberal economists? They were certainly not spokespeople or direct representatives of any of the pressure groups representing the various interests at stake in the business world. Over and above their social backgrounds, the personal links that they might have had with certain political parties, or their working relationship with specific firms or services, the decisive factor in the identity of the Chicago Boys is that they formed an ideological community based on their educational trajectories. As one of the group's best-known members puts it:

> Around the middle of the 1950s, the University of Chicago had initiated a program of academic exchange with the Catholic University in Chile, sending some of its professors to Chile to carry out research while at the same time receiving Chilean postgraduate students. By virtue of this program, accompanied by a system of grants, around one hundred students had completed their studies, graduating from the University of Chicago [during the 1960s and early 1970s]. . . . By 1972, many of these economists, back in Chile, entered the universities as full-time teachers. Others entered public posts, especially during the Frei government. The rest began to work for the major firms of the country but all formed a community, swelled every year by generations of new economists leaving Chilean universities, who shared a technical language, a rationalist approach to the solution of problems, and the desire to contribute with their efforts to the creation of a prosperous, just and free society. The majority of these economists are today—whether they like it or not—known as Chicago Boys.[12]

This "class" origin, linked to the possession of attributes and qualifications highly valued in the meritocratic culture of the Chilean middle class, became in itself an important factor in the group's ideological influence over the military establishment. Chile provides a contrast to other Latin American countries such as Argentina or Brazil, insofar as the upper ranks of the military (especially in the army) come overwhelmingly from the urban middle class and share its modernizing nature, opposed to the aristocratic features of upper-class landowners. The constitution of a community of economists with technical knowledge gave the discourse of this group a universalist appeal. It was precisely the element that was lacking in the particular discourses of the political parties as well as the various *gremios*, especially when dealing with an actor such as the military, which did not possess direct links with specific interest groups.[13]

On the other hand, the specific academic background of these economists was by no means irrelevant. The Department of Economics at the University of Chicago was unique within the North American academic community. Well known from the beginning for its theoretical conservatism and extreme neoclassicism, the department "kept alive the vision of a fundamental truth for a small circle of the initiated during the dark years of Keynesian despotism."[14] Chicago was a center of resistance in the face of the clear political and cultural hegemony enjoyed by Keynesian theory from the 1940s on. This has been described by Chicago's principal intellectual leader, Milton Friedman, in the introduction to *Capitalism and Freedom*: "Those of us who were profoundly worried by the danger to freedom and prosperity posed by the growth of government, the triumph of the welfare state and Keynesian ideas, made up a small minority and we were considered eccentric by the vast majority of our intellectual colleagues." Hence the agreement for academic collaboration with the Chilean Catholic University

reflected the efforts of a group of Chicago professors to protect the true science of economics, that is, orthodox neo-classical theory, from the socializing offensive of Keynesianism. During the epoch in which the agreements for collaboration were signed, the groups of the Chilean right were suffering from a profound hegemonic crisis, and the "mission" which was transmitted to Chile gave to those Chilean economists trained in Chicago the strength needed by groups who felt called upon to follow a revolutionary destiny.[15]

The task of extending the influence of these economists in Chilean society was not easy. They had to confront competition from a solid elite of economic professionals trained in the CEPAL structuralist school, whose headquarters in Santiago had been for decades a source of ideological dissemination to the intellectuals of the country. In addition, their policy prescriptions ran contrary to what had historically been, at least since the 1920s, the program of the political right, their natural ally, and of the business class. The break with democratic institutions, the subsequent removal of the influence of the political parties on government conduct, and the necessity of the military elite to find a longer-lasting source of legitimacy than that which could be provided by a simple program of "pacification" offered an unexpected opportunity for the unfolding of the "pure" plan of the Chicago economic school.

The early connections established between the military and the technical teams of the Christian Democrats tended to diminish and disappeared altogether when the party put political conditions on its participation—chiefly in terms of the life span of the regime and the calling of new general elections.[16] This opened the way for the neoliberal economists, insofar as it increased the independence of economic management from politics, but it still did not free that management from the pressures of the business associations.

As Campero points out, "The tradition . . . of the business *gremios* and, indeed, of their leadership was statist in practice. In fact, their development benefited in the 1920s, and above all in the 1940s, from state protection within the framework of import-substituting industrialization."[17] For this reason, although the experience of Popular Unity had led them to a more clearly antistatist position, the return of political security under an authoritarian anti-Marxist government encouraged business to press for protection of national industry.

The preoccupation of the organizations of big business with the growing power of the neoliberal technocracy in the spheres of government (and in particular its growing influence over the head of the junta, General Pinochet) was clearly manifest at the beginning of 1974 in a speech by the president of the powerful National Industrial Society: "Like all Chileans," he stated, alluding to the lack of influence of the business sector in drawing up economic policy,

> our knowledge of economic policy is limited to very broad principles. . . . A development model cannot be alien to the particular nature of the people who adopt it, nor run contrary to their physical and historical characteristics. . . . Economic achievements are only means of achieving certain political and social goals, but cannot be considered as ends in themselves. This is what distinguishes the

statesman from the technocrat: the former cannot be subjected to the latter.[18]

In the view of this important leader, a development strategy must be based on the following principles:

> Mixed economy, state firms only in high-risk strategic areas and the provision of "non-economic" services, the absolute necessity of planning as a mechanism for forecasting cyclical crises, opening up a competitive capital market, the entrance of foreign capital regulated by statutes to protect the national interest, appropriate use of tariffs to regulate national and international competition, and transformation of the traditional structure of the firm to allow the achievement of social development objectives, without which there will never be a social-market economy.[19]

Similar statements were made by small and medium organizations, which complained about lack of consultation with regard to the economic policies directly affecting them.

The absolute hegemony of the Chicago Boys was not, however, achieved overnight. It became evident only toward the end of 1975 and was symbolized by the withdrawal from the government of Minister for Economic Co-ordination Raúl Sáez and the application of a harsh policy of anti-inflationary shock by his successor, Jorge Cauas.

The 1974–75 crisis was the catalyst that led to the definitive transfer of leadership in economic policy from the business *gremios* to the civilian technocracy.[20] This crisis, in effect, led to the weakening of the principal factor that had allowed the business class to maintain a certain critical perspective on government decisions. The increasingly unstable economic situation began to lead to doubts concerning the political irreversibility of the military regime. The specter of an uncontrollable social explosion that would breathe life back into the defeated forces of Popular Unity led the business class to close ranks around the military and, in particular, around General Pinochet. The general, for his part, handed over all positions of economic responsibility to the neoliberal technocracy, also removing the navy from the position of responsibility for economic policy, which it had held under the division of labor introduced by the military junta in 1973. In this way, the crisis of 1974–75 marked an important milestone in the concentration of not only private economic power but also political power, arising from the civil-military rebellion of 1973, in the hands of an elite that was autonomous from immediate class considerations. As in any revolution worthy of the name, the social base that produced it was replaced by an elite that proclaimed itself to be the revolution's "guiding light."

The domination of these new actors during the period from 1975 until the crisis of 1982 permitted sustained transformation of the old economic order. The protectionist resistance that had been offered in varying degrees by the business *gremios* was broken, and the government economic team gave itself over completely to the task of opening the Chilean economy to the exterior, favoring the development of only those sectors that enjoyed comparative advantages over external competition. One basic instrument was a reduction in tariffs. Freeing up the capital markets and then completely opening to external financial flows constituted the principal institutional transformation that would prepare the way for massive privatizations.

It did not take long for the immediate consequences of these measures to become apparent to various business sectors. After the profound recession of 1974–75, the "reactivation" that began around 1976 was clearly selective. While the biggest wave of bankruptcies since the great crisis of 1929 swept the country, some firms from the primary export sector, and some involved in the processing of natural resources, began a slow process of advance. But the most notable feature of this period was that the liberalization of the capital market, as well as very high interest rates, encouraged an increasing shift of capital from the productive to the financial sector. Taking advantage of a highly profitable primary informal financial system and the elimination of restrictions on obtaining private foreign loans, the expected offspring of the antistatist model emerged: the large economic-financial groups, which were the first real actors in the private economy who sought to take a clear lead in the new order.

## The New Financial-Economic Groups

In an article written in the middle of the Chilean economic boom, Ricardo Lagos points out that what was novel about this period was not the existence of great private economic conglomerates.[21] These had always existed in the country, despite having been battered by the nationalization policy of Popular Unity. What was original was that the main groups are newcomers and they are nothing like their predecessors. Analysis of the groups from the past shows that they had their origin in activities involving productive goods—agriculture, industry or mining—and from there, they had expanded their interest to financial activities. . . . Moreover, these groups had a long history and trajectory.

The newly emerging groups, on the contrary,

have no historic roots and do not have their origin in the control of one or several firms linked to productive goods sectors, but rather in the control of financial activity. . . . The manipulation of the financial apparatus has allowed them to [buy up businesses and thus] bring new firms into the group, but up until the present, they have not created new ones. . . . The third characteristic is the high degree of centralization and control that they exert over the firms that they own. . . . The destiny of the assets of a particular firm, and its plans for expansion, are decided at a level far from the firm itself, and the executives of the firm have little say in the matter.

The "fourth and final characteristic," according to this author, is

the rapid expansion that such groups have undergone in the last seven years. There are no precise figures that allow us to extrapolate an annual growth rate. It is evident, however, that the change from a position of almost nothing, which was the situation prevailing in September 1973, to the current 1981 position implies a rhythm of expansion unheard of in Chile. Today, two of the principal groups control shares worth more than a thousand million, or one thousand five hundred million, dollars. Obviously, this has happened under very special conditions, but in any case, this is a highly unusual pattern. It is not just a matter of the "efficiency" of some with respect to others. It is something more.[22]

This "something more" was precisely the "visible hand" through which the state proposed to create a private economic power with the end—according to its expressed ideology—of "making the economy independent from politics." The discovery that new groups without historical roots were emerging testifies to the process that was taking place. It was not a case of consolidated socioeconomic actors who expressed themselves politically through this technocratic elite. On the contrary, the technocratic elite created conditions that were favorable for the emergence of new business leaders. These favorable conditions were rapidly capitalized upon by a few audacious businessmen.

The path that led to the constitution of these large financial-economic groups can be described fairly simply. First, with the majority of the banks still controlled by the public sector (the entire banking system had been taken under state control during Popular Unity), the state allowed the creation of financial societies. Given low liquidity and the existing restrictions on the operation of the banks, these financial societies achieved a rate of growth in their deposits and loans much higher than that of the banking system, in spite of the fact that their interest rates were notably higher. The strongest of these financial societies formed the embryo of the first groups. Toward the end of 1976, a severe crisis in the system (manifested in a growing number of bankruptcies and frauds) led to increased control by the Banking Supervisory Committee over the financial societies. The societies were divided into two groups, designated as "formal" (those that were subjected to this control) and "informal" (those that were not). Thus only the most powerful could stay in the market. Once private accumulation had reached important levels, the banks themselves were transferred by the government to the private sector, falling into the hands of the financial-economic groups that had accumulated rapidly in the earlier speculative period. Finally, the banks were given the capacity to obtain external credit. This led to an opening toward international financial capital and implied unequal internal competition, since firms owned by the groups had access to cheap external credit, thanks to the high international liquidity that was characteristic of the latter half of the 1970s. Firms not belonging to the groups had to borrow expensively from the banking system, which in any case was owned by these groups.

The relationship between these emerging private economic groups and the state technocratic elite—-in contrast to what happened with the *gremio* organizations of the businessmen—became extremely fluid. As Lagos has pointed out:

Two "classes" of executive have been emerging within the largest groups: the analysts and the managers. The role of the latter is well known; they are in charge of the firm and their role is to combine labor, capital, primary materials and other inputs and technology in order to produce a good or service. The analysts, on the other hand, observe the global progress of the Chilean economy and decide the expansion policy of the group, in timber, textiles, metallurgy, fruit exports—from mining production to production of foodstuffs—depending on their vision of the future of the national or international economy. In this process, the much reviled concept of planning has been extensively used, but within each group. This is a common process in advanced capitalist countries. It is strange that it was not much used in previous decades. Today these group analysts are planners but obviously in the interests of the group. It is the case of a bourgeoisie that uses and respects technical skill.[23]

In practice, it was the same technocratic leadership that circulated fluidly between management posts in the state and strategic advisory posts within private groups. This leadership not only created the conditions for the emergence of a new business faction but also modernized business management, displacing the historic power of traditional firms. These firms' "efficiency," which had been based on their capacity to influence the national state in order to achieve positions of competitive privilege in the internal market, lost all relevance within the framework of an open economy, in which new elites exercised great power.

There was still one fundamental element missing for the internal accumulation of capital, and the conditions that were to bring it about did not present themselves until 1978. The first primitive division of labor of the military junta, in which the navy took control of the economy, had left responsibility for social policy in the hands of the air force. From the beginning, given the critical tension that had existed in employer-worker relations under Popular Unity, the focus of attention in the social field was on labor policy. But since the battle with radical unionism was confined to the "political" area of the administration, labor policy reform concentrated on a more limited area of concern: employer-worker relations within the firm.

The first steps toward institutional reform in the field of labor relations were of a corporatist nature. The Ministry of Labor—originally headed by an air force general—tried to reestablish some contact with non-Marxist union organizations. This was in relation to four big projects for the redefinition of labor relations, which would reconstitute a powerful but depoliticized unionism, "associated" with the economic success of the firms. The projects included a preliminary plan for reforming the labor code that had been in force since 1931, a statute of social security, a statute of occupational training, and what was called the social statute of the firm. This latter was perhaps the most ambitious of the four and sought, among other things, to establish mechanisms for worker participation at the level of production. Such an effort enjoyed the firm support of the person with ultimate responsibility for social policy—the commander-in-chief of the air force and member of the military junta, Gustavo Leigh.

The "social projects" were presented formally at the beginning of 1975 and were reduced to only two of the original four: the social statute of the firm and the national training system. In spite of this, the air force generals who had participated in their elaboration insisted that the projects were part of a larger scheme. This would include a reform of the labor code with reference to workers' organizations and the process of collective negotiation, as well as a social security reform that would allow workers to "participate in the ownership of national wealth created through the investment of social security funds."[24]

Campero and Valenzuela argue that the presentation of these projects was indicative of the clash between two different outlooks within the military government.

Those heading social and labor policy (Gustavo Leigh and Nicanor Díaz Estrada respectively—both Air Force generals) accorded an importance to their projects which went much further than an examination of the specific contents might suggest. In effect, the final outline of the Social Statute of the Firm was simply a system which provided workers and employers with information on the functioning of the firm. The Training Statute gave more control to the employers than to the workers, although it did offer the latter some possibilities for technical training. In reality, the idea of Leigh and Díaz Estrada seems to have been directed towards defining a position that would counterbalance the liberal-capitalist proposals and the transnational framework that was growing increasingly strong within economic policy. In following this line, both military men seemed to be seeking social support from the workers for their more nationalistic and populist proposals, which were framed within a corporatist ideology. The gap was growing between the institutionalizing and populist policy of the social-labor sector within the government and economic policy.[25]

This conflict would be resolved once again by the centralization of political power in the hands of the commander-in-chief of the armed forces (and president of the junta), General Pinochet. After the presentation of the social and labor reforms, Pinochet took steps to ensure that they entered into long periods of study by commission (as in the case of the reforms to the labor code) or that they were never applied in spite of having been formally approved (as in the case of the social statute of the firm). The minister of labor, Díaz Estrada, resigned in February 1976 and was succeeded by a lawyer close to the positions of the neoliberal economic team, Sergio Fernández. Later, in 1978, General Leigh was sacked from his position as commander-in-chief of the air force in an audacious show of strength (which also swept into retirement most of the generals in that branch of the armed forces).[26]

After a brief period of compromise, Pinochet named the Harvard-trained economist José Piñera as the new minister of labor, thereby opening the way for his young free-market technocrats to redefine social policy. The appointment of Piñera marked the beginning of an extensive and radical attempt by the neoliberal technocracy to transform the country's social institutions. This is graphically represented by Valdés as a moment in which the elite of economists had "utopia within arm's reach." Not only the new institutionalism and economic policy, but the whole social structure of the country opened up as a potential field for experimentation, based upon the pure truth of rational choice and the calculus of marginal utility. And although the price of this experiment was the acceptance of dictatorship, it was a price worth paying, as Piñera himself made clear in a statement that (with its affirmation of the *volonté générale*) brings to mind both Lenin and Robespierre: "Although it is clear that these reforms cannot be carried out under the traditional rules of the political game, the majority of citizens give the government their support so that it can meet its objectives."[27]

A program was set in motion that received the Maoist-sounding title of "The Plan of Seven Modernizations." The most important of these related to the reform of labor relations, the social security system, and the two principal areas of public social spending, health and education.

The labor reforms proposed to legalize union organizations, starting from the principle of "union freedom." Within each firm any number of unions could exist, providing they satisfied the requirement for a minimum number of workers. Each worker had the right to withdraw from a union or not to join any union. Intersectoral collective bargaining was not permitted, and wage agreements had to be related to productivity to make them "technical" and not transform them into "a mechanism for the redistribution of wealth." The union had to be a form of social and technical, but not political, participation. Federations and confederations would be allowed only an advisory role. The right to strike was permitted, but with a maximum duration of sixty days, and the employer was entitled to declare a lockout or sack workers under the pretext of promoting the good of the firm. The minimum wage was abolished in 1979, along with the employer's obligation to pay social security costs for youth and apprentices (measures designed to "introduce flexibility into the labor market in the interest of workers," since high pension costs and minimum wage legislation tended to favor unemployment). In its original form, allowance was made for an automatic annual wage adjustment to take account of inflation, but this was never applied and was formally revoked a year later.

The most far-reaching reform, however, was that of the social security system. The system prevailing in Chile for four decades was one that corresponded to the "solidarity sharing system" of collective contributions run by the state, under which active workers financed nonactive workers with a theoretically egalitarian distribution of the benefits. "The 'modernization' of national insurance schemes consisted of principles that ran exactly contrary to those previously existing. Individual contributions replaced collective ones, the level of protection was determined by the income level of the person insured, and pension funds were transferred to 'private hands,' a euphemism for the Pension Administration Funds (AFP) set up by individual economic groups."[28] This reform had an enormous impact on the abilities of the financial-economic groups to raise capital. According to calculations by José Pablo Arellano, at the time the system was introduced, social security contributions made up a sum of resources equivalent to 20 percent of all the deposits in current accounts of the entire national banking and financial system.[29]

Reforms with a similar inspiration were implemented in the field of health care with the creation of Institutes of Health Insurance (ISAPRES), which allowed employees to authorize the transfer of health insurance funds (which had previously been channeled into provincial health services) into private programs. This measure was accompanied by a notable decline in finance for the public health system, leading to a massive transfer of funds from better-off workers—particularly administrative employees—to the private sector.

In the area of education, a less radical reform transferred to the municipalities the administration of publicly financed educational establishments and the negotiation of contracts for teaching staff (which had previously been centralized in the Ministry of Education).

The philosophy that guided these transformations was simple and would acquire a greater consistency in the future, when the old National Planning Office (ODEPLAN) emerged as a new center for the neoliberal technocracy and took control of social policy. The argument was that the state should concentrate its efforts exclusively on the poorest sectors of the population, targeting them for social spending. The greater the reduction in expenditures on public bureaucracy, the more the tax burden of firms could be reduced, favoring investment. This would lead to more opportunities for employment, and the population with the least resources would then be able to escape from poverty, pulling themselves up by their own bootstraps.[30]

The refounding of society did not stop at this point, however. The philosophical enthusiasm of the economists contributed decisively to the military effort to institutionalize and legitimize the power of General Augusto Pinochet. This occurred through a new political constitution, subject once again to a controversial referendum in the form of a "plebiscite" in 1979 and coming into operation the following year.

By 1980, then, the influence of the three principal architects of the new Chilean reality was approaching its zenith. Virtually all political power was concentrated in the hands of General Pinochet. Thanks to this total power, the neoliberal economists were able to impose their free-market economic model on all public economic and social institutions. And as a result of the institutional conditions generated by these actors, financial-economic groups faced no opposition to their domination of the domestic market. In the face of this implacable triangle, and in the middle of the boom led by the firms belonging to the principal groups (and a growing capacity for consumption among high- and middle-income groups), the old corporate organizations of the business sector had to retreat into adaptive or supportive strategies. This framework would be modified only by the great crisis provoked by the recession of 1982–83.

## A Corporate Interlude

The 1982 crisis had its origin in the insolvency of the edifice constructed by the financial-economic groups and was precipitated by a high level of debt, coupled with the increased price of external credit and a declining market for exports caused by the international crisis. The monopolistic activity of the groups was called into question by a large section of the business community, who saw themselves as having been dragged into the crisis by the domino effect that the bankruptcy of certain leading firms transmitted to the banks and other productive sectors.

The most immediate reaction came from the small and medium businesses, grouped since the end of the 1970s in the Confederation of Small and Medium Companies. Toward the middle of 1982, these *gremios*—particularly in the southern provinces of the country—began to move from partial criticism of economic policy to active mobilization. They openly criticized government support of the economic groups. The leaders of larger companies, albeit more reluctantly, concluded that the crisis was not of a transitory nature and urged the government to follow a more pragmatic and less ideological economic policy. This meant restricting the autonomy of the technocrats and arriving at negotiated measures with the business associations. To the pressure from the *gremios* that arose from the economic crisis would be added, the following year, the social and political emergency unleashed by the social protests discussed in chapter 1. After the golden age that had begun in the postcrisis period of 1976, the three pillars of the government elite were increasingly threatened with checkmate.

The elite controlling government and the process of socioeconomic transformation was faced with three types of challenge. The first was a massive social rebellion, headed by a reborn political opposition demanding the end of the military regime. The second was the effort made by leaders of small and medium firms to revitalize the old *gremio* organizations and mobilize them to offset the direction taken by the technocratic economic team within the government. The third was that posed by the principal business leaders of the country, grouped in the Confederation of Production and Commerce, who sought to negotiate a pragmatic program to overcome the crisis, involving a reorientation of the growth strategy that would not endanger the overall market nature of the economy.

Changes to the power structure followed swiftly. At the end of 1981, confronted with a critical situation reflected in the overdue loans of many banks and financial societies, the government decided to intervene in eight of these credit institutions in order to prevent a general collapse of the financial system. At the same time, an army general (Luis

Danús) with greater powers of intervention in the economy was designated as director of ODEPLAN, while José Piñera was removed from his post as minister of mining. At the start of 1982, Pinochet dismissed the intellectual leader of the Chicago Boys in Chile, Sergio de Castro, from the Ministry of Finance (replacing him, nevertheless, with another technocrat of similar stamp but less influence). The policy of maintaining a fixed exchange rate against the dollar, implemented between 1979 and 1982 as an essential part of the idea of "automatic adjustment," was replaced with continuous devaluations of the peso. General Luis Danús moved from ODEPLAN to occupy the Ministry of the Economy. Around the middle of 1983, as an immediate consequence of the social protests, Sergio Fernández—a principal ally of the neoliberal technocracy—was replaced as minister of the interior by veteran national-corporatist politician Sergio Onofre Jarpa. Together with new ministers in the economic field, he was closely linked to the pragmatic orientation of major companies. Faced with a situation that would require compromise and negotiation, as much with political sectors as with social ones, Pinochet assumed a certain distance from policymaking. This was an attitude similar to that of a president in a parliamentary system, giving responsibility to his new minister of the interior, Jarpa, for the decisions adopted.

Nevertheless, this period represented a brief interlude in the exercise of power without counterweight by Pinochet and his young technocrats in government. The first challenge, of social protest, as has already been shown, lost its immediate explosive force with the increasingly routine nature of the protests, although it would lead to the defeat of the regime in the medium term. The second challenge was from the small and medium businesses that had felt close to victory with the designation of Jarpa to head the cabinet.[31] Their attempts at mobilization and pressure, nevertheless, were overcome through separate negotiations on the demands of various sectors and did not lead in any degree to an organic incorporation of the old *gremio* movement into the military government. The final challenge, represented by big business sectors who sought to negotiate a global program for economic policy, was met by a refusal on the part of the government to give in. It responded only with "segmented and gradual responses to specific demands."[32]

The reason for this new strength on the part of the governing elite, which quickly allowed it to become independent again from the business *gremios* and to do away with the veteran politicians in the cabinet, was the recomposition of the civil technocracy under a new leadership (that of the engineer Hernán Büchi). The latter was then capable of giving a coherent response to the three great problems facing the economy: the renegotiation and payment of the external debt, the crisis in the national financial system, and the crisis of credibility in the overall economic model.

Above all, the crisis did away with the model of the "minimum state," characterized by its passivity in the business sphere, and led to a phase dominated by an "active state." This involved the renegotiation of debt, as well as new external loans to cover the interest payments that could not be rescheduled, and led to an agreement with the International Monetary Fund for a new deflationary adjustment that combined a restriction on global demand with a reorientation of the growth strategy. To this end, an active role for the state emerged, designed to increase internal savings and investment, expand exports, and achieve a series of macroeconomic targets (involving net international reserves, new external loans, tariff and exchange rate policy, maximum nonfinancial public-sector deficit, maximum inflation rate, and wage policies). The agreements with the Fund were certainly helpful for the technocratic elite in the face of the expansionary proposals of the business associations.

The confidence of the principal business leaders in the managers of economic policy recovered rapidly, thanks to unwavering state assistance to the large debtors during the crisis.[33] The external debt, for the most part run up by private agents without state guarantees, became a public responsibility when the state stepped in to guarantee the overdue loans of the private sector. The setting up of a "preferential dollar" for external debtors signified a transfer of public funds to these agents of 35 percent of the value of their debts, to which was added the possibility of "dedollarizing" external debts. This unique form of state intervention in favor of the business class was also evident in the handling of internal debt. Successive state interventions in banks and financial societies meant that 64 percent of these institutions' capital and reserves came under public control. So did a significant part of the productive system (owing to the fact that a large number of bankrupt firms passed into the hands of the creditor banks, and hence to the state, which had intervened in the latter). This interventionist wave, however, which allowed the state to accumulate an economic power even greater than that of the government during the nationalizing period of Popular Unity, was quickly followed—as soon as the economic indicators showed signs of recovery—by a new and even more drastic wave of reprivatizations that returned the firms ("cleansed" by fiscal aid) to private hands and included other important firms that had historically been part of the public sector.

The policy followed as a result of the crisis led to the selective reconstitution of the internal economic groups and a new form of association between these groups and foreign capital. On the one hand, the main purchasers of firms in this second wave of privatizations were the pension administration funds created in the period before the crisis. By the end of 1985, these funds controlled resources equivalent to more than 10 percent of GDP. On the other hand, the formula of capitalization used to overcome the problem of external debt (which consisted of allowing foreign investors to buy bonds in the market for Chilean foreign debt, which they could then use for investment purposes within the country by exchanging them for shares in private or public companies) meant a new injection of capital that went, principally, to the pension administration funds. Foreign investors were attracted by the funds' rules forbidding risky investments, which constituted protection against the kind of speculative spiral that had led to the crash of 1982.

Having overcome both the immediate political emergency of the protests of 1983 and the most serious debt problems (which had prompted larger business *gremios* to pressure for greater participation in economic decisionmaking, and small and medium businesses to call for the replacement of the management team), both Pinochet and the civil neoliberal technocracy regained incontestable power. Figures from the wider world of politics and business who had joined the cabinet during the most severe moments of the crisis, and who had aroused hopes among leaders of business *gremios* that they might have a voice in the military government, quickly disappeared. As Pinochet would graphically put it later, drawing on an image from boxing, this period had simply been a case of sidestepping to recover strength.

## The Decline of the Elite

The stubborn tendency of the elite in power to seek autonomy from the class that supported it explains the radical nature of the transformations at work in Chilean society. These transformations helped to generate (through the state, as in the dreams of many great reformers) a new civil society; and this allows one to understand another salient feature of the Chilean experience, which was the peaceful nature of its political transition to democratic rule.

The very success in the creation of new general rules for social life, particularly the reduction of direct economic state power, increased the advantages for the business sector of having political management undertaken on a predominantly administrative basis, rather than by an elite guided by a foundational logic. The persistence of the elite increased the risks of widespread political conflict and cyclical economic crises, which could signify a permanent game of "all or nothing"—a game that is easily accepted when one is close to having nothing, but not quite so readily when one is close to having all.

As already mentioned, although the social and political opposition to the military government had not achieved its immediate objectives by insurrectional means in the protests of 1983, it had managed to develop a growing movement geared toward the defeat of Pinochet by political means. In the absence of other alternatives, this meant that attention was focused on the plebiscite scheduled for 1988.

For these reasons the leaders of the business *gremios*, although they continued until the last day to give their support to the military government they had helped to install, also began, with the passing of the 1983 crisis, to extend their independence with respect to this power elite. Until the crisis, their only dialogue had been with the military government; following the crisis, they opened up channels of communication with the big union branches and opposition political parties. This was with the perspective of developing what was called a process of "social cooperation." At the same time, the old political right, which following the military coup had agreed voluntarily to dissolve its party structures, began to reestablish them publicly, in order to "support but not form part of the government." Thus, while Pinochet returned to the center of the ring following his neat footwork, ready to knock out or be knocked out, members of the public were already buying their tickets for the next fight. The autonomy of the elite following the crisis of 1983 would be the last that the restructured Chilean capitalist class would accept for reasons of "emergency."

Something similar was taking place in the sphere of military support for the government. The air force, the navy, and even the militarized police, which over the years had suffered the blows attendant upon the centralization of all power in the hands of the commander-in-chief of the army, emphasized their support for the institutional transition established by the 1980 constitution. They would stick by Pinochet until the 1988 plebiscite, but they would not be disposed to follow him in any type of coup attempt if he lost.

These were the last moments of a situation in which the governing elite could dominate the class that had supported it. This domination had been based upon the lack of a national project that would give voice to the political and social aspirations of business, as well as the continual presentation of catastrophic alternatives in which everything that had been won could be lost in a moment. The old business organizations and the reborn parties of the political right were outdone until the last day by the strength of General Pinochet and his economists. Tellingly, the presidential plebiscite included Pinochet as the candidate, in spite of the public lack of enthusiasm manifested by the majority of rightist politicians. The following year, the presidential candidate of the bloc that had supported the military government was Hernán Büchi, who had led the neoliberal technocracy through the crisis of 1983.

But the defeat of both was not a defeat for the business class. The military returned to the barracks, the Chicago Boys to managing the most important financial-economic groups in the country, and the old organizations of employers to speaking for themselves again. The dialogue between the business *gremios* and the majority right-wing political party, on the one hand, with the unions, political parties, and government of the Democratic Coalition on the other, has been a key to the orderly nature of the Chilean political transition.

# 4

# Restructuring and the New Working Classes

During the decade from 1982 to 1992, the social structure of Chile was fundamentally transformed, particularly in relation to the condition of workers and the nature of poverty. The central thesis of this study is that the breakup of the old social structure, which was the most important feature of the period from 1973 to 1982, has been completed. This was a period characterized by rising unemployment, a fall in waged work, a growth in urban informal employment, and an increase in marginality. By contrast, 1982–92 was a period of social restructuring, which speeded up after 1986, and was marked by falling unemployment, a reduction in informal and tertiary (services) employment, and an increase in waged work.

Examination of what took place between 1973 and 1992 leads to the conclusion that a real historical cycle of destructuring and restructuring has occurred. This is similar to what took place in Chile between 1920 and 1940—a period that encompassed the nitrate crisis and the Ibáñez del Campo dictatorship, lasting until the Popular Front and the beginnings of import-substituting industrialization. Nevertheless, the cycle that would seem to have just ended has had a wider spatial impact, a different structural direction, and a greater susceptibility to future changes and fluctuations. This is because the Chilean economy is more open, and hence sectors and regions are susceptible to more rapid and intense situations of expansion or decline than was the case at the middle of the century.

The direction and magnitude of change cannot fail to impress the observer. In the last three-month period of 1982, more than 1.2 million people were unemployed or participating in emergency work programs.

101

Ten years later, the number of unemployed had been reduced to less than 250,000, at the same time that the emergency work programs had ceased and informal urban employment had experienced a relative decline. This means that between 1982 and 1992 more than a million Chileans left the ranks of the unemployed at the same time that under-employment was falling. Of course, the official statistics are generous in their understanding of what constitutes an employed person.[1] It is nevertheless undeniable that the rate of unemployment has been sub-stantially reduced, from 27 percent in 1982 to 4.4 percent in 1992.

The consolidation of the newly emerging economy and social struc-ture has coincided with the democratization of the country. This has opened the way for a subjective reshaping of Chilean society, whose characteristics will take years to acquire a more definitive form. In the meantime, it is important to document and analyze the major trends of change occurring within the world of work. That is the purpose of this chapter.

## The New Waged Employment

During the 1980s, various sociological and economic studies pointed to a process of falling waged employment in the developed industrial world, without paying sufficient attention to notable exceptions such as Japan and the newly industrializing countries of Southeast Asia. There was a tendency to view this phenomenon as a global process that was being extended to Latin America. The origins of the process were seen to lie in structural crisis, as well as the transition toward a new eco-nomic model in which the so-called wage relation loses importance.[2] By the same token, workers as a different social group and relevant social actors also become less significant in the political system.

### Emerging Trends

During 1973–83 Chile appeared to have followed the same road, as illustrated in figure 4-1. There was a reduction in the relative and absolute importance of waged workers, as much in the middle as in the working class.[3] Waged work fell during 1972–83 from 65.7 percent to 48.2 percent of total employment.[4] This decline was intimately related to two economic crises, the first in 1974–75 and the second in 1982–83. Between 1979 and 1983, the total number of waged workers fell from 1.9 million to 1.4 million. Half of this reduction can be explained by a drastic reduction in public employment ( − 75,000) and a major

FIGURE 4-1.  *Waged Workers, as Percentage of Employed Population,*
*1976–94*

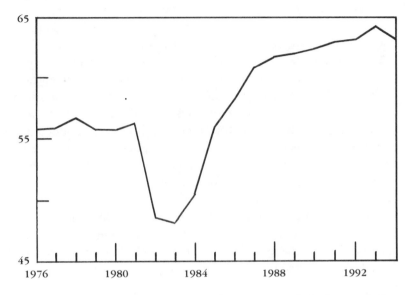

SOURCE: National Statistical Institute of Chile, National Employment Survey. Data are for fourth quarter of each year.

decrease in industrial employment ( − 65,000). The origin of this rapid
decline in waged employment was the fierce neoliberal structural adjustment that aggravated the consequences of two external shocks
(1974–75 and 1981–83) and generated deep recession and massive
unemployment in the tradable goods sector (for example, the manufacturing industry). This impact was deepened by the drastic rationalization of public employment.

Nevertheless, between 1983 and 1992 the evidence shows a reversal
in this process. During that period employment increased by 1.8 million
people, 86 percent of whom were waged. By the beginning of 1987, the
rate of waged work was higher than in 1980–81 (the years before the
1982–83 recession), and by 1992 this rate stood at 63.1 percent of total
employment, which was also higher than in 1966 and almost the same
as in 1970.[5]

At the same time, it is important to note that although the proportion
of the labor force in waged work increased between 1982 and 1992,
the same did not occur with the share of wages in national income,
which remained stationary at around 38 percent. Here it should be
pointed out that the fall in waged work in the previous period (1975–

82) was accompanied by a considerable increase in the concentration of personal income, and that the rebound in waged work did not reverse the situation. Currently, the richest 10 percent of the population controls 40 percent of disposable personal income—a situation that does not appear to have changed significantly since 1988.

The explanation for this phenomenon lies in two major groups of factors. First, there are structural factors involving the concentration of wealth in Chile's small open economy. These have their origin in the enhanced weight of large companies that produce or distribute the majority of exports. Around fifteen companies now control 85 percent of exports. The majority produce primary goods on a large scale with continuous production and a high capital-labor ratio. Second, there are institutional factors that have to do with the organization and control of capital markets and facilitate the concentration of surpluses. Furthermore, the organization of the labor market leads to its segmentation and to the massive presence of precarious employment. The weak bargaining power of labor has consistently meant that the growth of productivity per person-hour has been superior to the growth of real wages per hour.

At the same time, it should be pointed out that this situation is not necessarily permanent. The Chilean economy is growing, within the context of a type of real change that is qualitatively different from that which has taken place in the past. There is a progressive development of manufacturing industry and productive services. To that must be added a certain tightness in the labor market, the widening of negotiation and collective bargaining, and the future institutional reforms that will take place in a more advanced stage of democratic transition. All of this should feed through into a gradual but progressive increase in the share of wages in national income.

## The New Working Class(es)

Overall evidence invites the formulation of various different hypotheses about the social and political impact of the renewed growth in waged work. A basically structuralist approach could identify such a trend with the inevitable return of the working class to the political and social arena, perhaps in the form of union movements with the potential to influence the parties of center and left by reinforcing their class discourse and representation. This would strengthen the organic nature of civil society, creating a space for the rebirth of what was formerly known as the "compromising state" in Chile—an arrangement for the representation and reconciliation of conflicting interests that is both necessary and possible in a small open economy. Depending on the standpoint from which this is analyzed, such a possibility either fans old fears or revives old desires.

But this is simply one of several possibilities, the realization of which depends on a variety of political, social, and cultural factors. In fact, an analysis of the return to waged work leads to the conclusion that this does not entail the reproduction of the past at all, but rather the creation of very different structures of social relations. The roots of some of these can be outlined as follows.

CHANGES IN THE GENDER COMPOSITION OF THE LABOR FORCE. A notable departure from the past involves changes in the gender composition of the waged work force in Chile. Although women constitute a clear minority, their share has grown markedly, from 15.9 percent in 1966 to 27.6 percent in 1992. Waged women's share of total female employment has also risen, from 42.7 percent to 58.6 percent between 1966 and 1992. This increase is accounted for by the growth of waged female labor in the primary and tertiary sectors, which contrasts with a decline in the secondary sector.

SECTORAL CHANGES. Table 4-1 compares the position of waged work over a series of three-year periods: 1976–78, the first years of neoliberal structural adjustment within the context of an authoritarian regime and the beginning of an economic recovery; 1982–84, years of recession and high unemployment before the second structural adjustment of a more unorthodox type; and 1990-92, years of economic expansion within the context of transition and democratic government. Comparing the situation between 1976–78 and 1990–92, it is apparent that although shifts in the distribution of waged work among economic sectors have not been very large, significant changes have indeed occurred within sectors.

In the primary sector, there was a doubling of waged workers in agriculture (including forestry), between 1976–78 and 1990–92. The growth trend continued even during the crisis of 1982–84, reflecting the dynamics of modernization in the Chilean countryside. At the same time, the proportion of all waged work in the country that could be attributed to the agroforestry sector increased from 14 percent to 16 percent.

In the secondary sector, waged work in construction almost tripled, although this grew at an inferior rate to total employment in the sector.

TABLE 4-1. *Population in Waged Employment, by Sector, Selected Periods, 1976–92*[a]

| Sector | 1976–78 | | 1982–84 | | 1990–92 | |
|---|---|---|---|---|---|---|
| | Thousands | Percent | Thousands | Percent | Thousands | Percent |
| *Primary* | 297 | 19 | 293 | 19 | 558 | 19 |
| Agriculture | 219 | 14 | 227 | 15 | 458 | 16 |
| Fishing | 10 | ... | 15 | 1 | 20 | 1 |
| Mining | 69 | 4 | 52 | 3 | 80 | 3 |
| *Secondary* | 469 | 29 | 420 | 27 | 848 | 30 |
| Manufacturing industry | 356 | 22 | 318 | 20 | 595 | 21 |
| Utilities | 29 | 2 | 24 | 2 | 22 | 1 |
| Construction | 84 | 5 | 78 | 5 | 231 | 8 |
| *Tertiary* | 834 | 52 | 843 | 54 | 1,477 | 51 |
| Commerce | 191 | 12 | 243 | 16 | 406 | 14 |
| Transportation/ communication | 134 | 8 | 129 | 8 | 209 | 7 |
| Financial services | 60 | 4 | 85 | 5 | 181 | 6 |
| Other services | 180 | 11 | 170 | 11 | 491 | 17 |
| Public employment | 270 | 17 | 215 | 14 | 190 | 7 |
| Total | 1,601 | 100 | 1,556 | 100 | 2,883 | 100 |

SOURCE: National Statistical Institute of Chile (INE), National Employment Survey, fourth quarter.
a. Three-year averages.

Not surprisingly, opportunities for waged employment have also increased markedly in those areas of manufacturing industry directly linked to the processing of natural resources. Activities in industries such as textiles and metallurgy have, however, declined in importance.

In general, the tertiary (or services) sector has shown a pattern of increase in waged work, a process that slowed down with the crisis but accelerated during the second half of the 1980s. Between the beginning and the end of the period under discussion, the rate of waged employment within the sector rose from 50 percent to 58 percent (although, as noted in table 4-1, the proportion of all waged labor in the country attributable to the tertiary sector remained almost constant). What is particularly striking is that the growing importance of waged labor relations within this sector took place despite an absolute decline in public employment, which fell by 30 percent, and as a share of the total waged work force declined from 17 percent to 7 percent.

At the same time, the number of waged workers in commerce doubled, a trend toward growth that continued even during the 1982–84 recession. Salaried employees in finance tripled over the whole period, a process that was temporarily stalled during 1982–84 when the crisis

TABLE 4-2 *Urban and Rural Waged Work, Selected Periods, 1976–92*[a]

| Type of employment | 1976–78 | 1982–84 | 1990–92 |
|---|---|---|---|
| *National employment* | | | |
| Index of total employment | 100 | 111 | 160 |
| Index of total waged work | 100 | 94 | 174 |
| Rate of waged work (percent) | 58 | 44 | 62 |
| *Urban employment* | | | |
| Index of urban employment | 100 | 113 | 173 |
| Index of waged employment | 100 | 113 | 186 |
| Rate of waged work (percent) | 61 | 45 | 64 |
| *Rural employment* | | | |
| Index of rural employment | 100 | 103 | 112 |
| Index of waged employment | 100 | 83 | 113 |
| Rate of waged work (percent) | 47 | 39 | 49 |
| Rural employment/total employment (percent) | 22 | 22 | 15 |
| Rural waged/total waged (percent) | 18 | 18 | 12 |
| *Agricultural employment (excluding fishing)* | | | |
| Index of total employment | 100 | 98 | 167 |
| Index of waged work | 100 | 103 | 229 |
| Rate of waged work (percent) | 44 | 47 | 55 |
| Agricultural employment/total employment (percent) | 18 | 16 | 19 |
| Agricultural waged/total waged (percent) | 13 | 12 | 17 |
| *Rural employment/agricultural employment* | | | |
| Rural employment/agricultural employment (percent) | 118 | 123 | 79 |
| Rural waged/agricultural waged (percent) | 129 | 108 | 70 |

SOURCE: National Statistical Institute of Chile (INE), National Employment Survey, fourth quarter.
a. Three-year averages.

directly affected the financial sector of the Chilean economy. Between 1976–78 and 1990–92, the two sectors increased their relative weight from 16 percent to 20 percent of the total waged labor force.

SHIFTS BETWEEN URBAN AND RURAL AREAS.  Between 1976 and 1992, there were important changes in the spatial distribution of waged workers. Urban employment grew more quickly than rural employment, reflecting a process of urbanization that reduced the absolute number of residents and size of the labor force in the rural areas. As can be seen in table 4-2, both total and waged rural employment declined as a percentage of national employment, while within rural areas themselves the proportion of the work force receiving salaries or wages grew less than that in urban areas.

Nevertheless, waged relations were extended in the countryside, and there is reason to think that the proportion of waged work in agriculture and fishing may be underestimated. In the first place, it would appear that many rural workers categorized as self-employed are, in reality, waged pieceworkers. In the second place, table 4-2 reveals a growing spatial asymmetry between place of residence and work in the agricultural sector, since an increasing proportion of those who work in the countryside live in urban areas. This is especially so for temporary workers who currently live in small and intermediate cities.

The indicators are extremely revealing in this respect. Between 1976 and 1992, the proportion of total employment represented by rural employment fell from 22 percent to 15 percent. Nevertheless, agricultural employment (excluding fishing) increased its relative importance in total employment and even more so in waged employment. In 1976–78 and 1982–84 there were more workers in the rural sector than in the agricultural sector. This was reversed in the second half of the 1980s and is reflected in the figures for 1990–92, suggesting an average of 680,000 people in rural employment and 800,000 in agricultural employment (excluding fishing). Such a process was (as noted above) concomitant with a reduction in the total population and labor force of rural areas.

It is clear that this is related to the expansion and diversification of agriculture and agro-industrial production, which is concentrated in terms of product and employment in the central valley. Between 1976 and 1992, waged employment fell in the northern and southern regions but grew in the central valley and extreme south.

SPATIAL DECENTRALIZATION.   Between 1976 and 1992, there was an increase of 1.4 million waged workers in Chile. Forty-three percent of this increase took place in Santiago and 10 percent in the two next largest cities (Valparaíso and Concepción), while 24 percent is explained by growth in intermediate cities, 21 percent in other urban areas, and 2 percent in rural areas. Thus although the bulk of the expansion of the waged labor force was concentrated in urban areas, a significant change occurred in the tendencies in previous decades for growth in waged labor to be concentrated almost exclusively in the three largest cities. Although more than 50 percent of waged workers continue to be concentrated in .these cities, their relative importance has decreased and the proportion of the labor force in waged labor has become more uniform between large, medium, and small cities. This reflects a structural change in the geography of waged labor in the country.

FIGURE 4-2.  *Employers and Waged Workers, 1976–94*

1976 = 100

SOURCE: National Statistical Institute of Chile, National Employment Survey. Data are for fourth quarter of each year.

In general, the proportion of all waged work in Chile that is carried out in urban areas has grown continuously over the past few decades, increasing from 70 percent to 84 percent of the total between 1970 and 1990.

DISPERSION OF WAGED WORKERS AMONG MORE FIRMS.   The Chilean business class underwent a double process of change over the 1980s. On the one hand, there was the reconstitution of powerful national economic groups and the entrance of foreign corporate interests, strengthened in both instances by the privatization of state enterprises. On the other hand, there was an expansion of small and medium business.

This expansion was not equally spread across sectors. In order of importance, greater growth was registered in the primary sector than in the secondary and tertiary sectors. The urban concentration of business increased, with a reduction in Santiago but a significant increase in the intermediate cities of Concepción and Valparaíso.

Figure 4-2 illustrates the dramatic growth in number of employers registered by national employment statistics over the past decade. Although during the period of economic recuperation that lasted from

1976 to 1980 there had been little growth either in employers or in waged workers, this situation changed completely from 1983 on. The number of employers tripled in the following decade, and the number of waged workers doubled. Since the numerical expansion of the business class was registered principally in small and medium firms, it is not unreasonable to suppose that a good part of the growth in waged work also took place in this type of enterprise. This would suggest a process of deconcentration or dispersion of waged workers among firms.[6]

## The New Informality

A great deal of attention has been paid by social scientists to the "informalization" of the economy in both industrial and developing countries. The concept tends to be used in two ways that are in some respects similar but in others quite different. The first bases analysis of informality on the expansion of certain types of economic relations that, either owing to a crisis or the dominant mode of regulation of the economy, constitute areas where the state intervenes in a weak or diffuse manner. The second, which is widely adopted, sees informality as a body of agents with certain characteristics who are located in the urban world. This latter concept tends to be expressed in terms of an urban informal sector.

Each usage of the term "informality" is associated with a distinct theoretical tradition. The first is currently employed within regulation theory, where agents appear in a complex world of economic relations. The second, focusing on the urban informal sector, is closely related to structural dualism. There are, however, still further differences of emphasis within the second camp. Some authors have understood the urban informal sector as a social system different from the formal economy, but subordinated to the latter through relations of unequal exchange.[7] This idea is a long way from theories that use the concept of a marginal mass that is presumed to be afunctional to the general system.[8]

In the Chilean case, various arguments have been put forward to explain the expansion of the urban informal sector. One highlights growing rural-urban migration, whether because of the incapacity of the rural world to absorb the growth in the economically active population or because of the attractiveness for the peasant of the differential between rural and urban wages.[9] Another emphasizes low demand for labor in the modern urban sector, owing to the technologies employed there.[10] There is also the suggestion that growth of the informal sector is linked to the crisis of the Chilean welfare state, which during the 1960s partially covered the urban world. In this argument, the increasing incapacity of the state to guarantee indirect wages promoted the development of alternative survival strategies within the low-income sectors. Such a process has been functional to capitalism, since it reduces the costs of reproducing the labor force. Finally, another important school of thought has argued that the successive recessions of 1974–75 and 1982–83, as well as neoliberal policy, have led to processes of deindustrialization and "spurious" service-sector activity, or "tertiarization." The latter is understood to involve hidden unemployment and to constitute a refuge for labor displaced from other sectors.[11]

It is well known that statistical problems can seriously distort any analysis of the urban informal sector. A strict definition of the sector includes self-employed workers, unwaged family members, and waged workers in microenterprises (employing one to five workers) and excludes domestic workers, as well as technical, professional, and managerial staff.[12] Nevertheless, given that information with respect to waged workers in microenterprises is not available, a more restricted definition of the urban informal sector, which includes only the self-employed and unpaid family labor, is generally used. (The exclusions already mentioned are maintained in this latter case.)

### Stagnation of Informal Employment

In Chile, the popularization of the term led to the impression that the urban informal sector was expanding in the long term, especially in the services sector, despite the fact that a study of the sector for 1960–80 pointed to the contrary.[13] Using the more restricted definition, it can be seen that the censuses of 1960, 1970, and 1982 reveal a progressive decline in the importance of the urban informal sector with respect to the urban working population as a whole. Using other available information, it is possible to show that it was during the 1970s that the urban informal sector grew more rapidly than urban employment as a whole (see table 4-3). This occurred not only because of the recession in 1974–75, but also because the type of recovery between 1976 and 1980 did not provide for a significant increase in employment in sectors like industry.[14] Nevertheless, during the 1980s the urban informal sector—in its restricted definition—grew at a lower rate than the urban working population. As a consequence, the Chilean case is not congruent with traditional explanations of a rise in informality.

TABLE 4-3. *Average Annual Rates of Growth in the Urban Informal Sector, Selected Periods, 1960–90*

| Period | Total population | Urban employment | Urban informal |
|---|---|---|---|
| 1960–70 | 2.04 | 2.35 | 1.63 |
| 1970–80 | 2.23 | 4.07 | 5.01 |
| 1980–90 | 1.56 | 3.17 | 2.77 |

SOURCE: Alvaro Díaz, "La reestructuración industrial autoritaria en Chile," *Revista Proposiciones* 17 (SUR, 1989), based on data from INE and PREALC.

A more detailed analysis for 1976–94 is provided in figure 4-3, which suggests that in Chile informality is procyclical and that between 1988 and 1994 it was below the levels of 1979–81. Nevertheless, it is obvious from the preceding discussion that the urban informal sector is underestimated here, since it is not possible to include waged workers, in particular those of micro-industries, in the database utilized to create figure 4-3. Taking account of this factor, one can at least conclude that the makeup of the urban informal sector has changed. The relative importance of self-employed workers and unpaid family labor has declined, while the importance of waged workers has increased. And given the expansion of waged work in Chile, it could be argued that

FIGURE 4-3. *Urban Informal Sector, 1976–94*

SOURCE: National Statistical Institute of Chile, National Employment Survey. Data are for fourth quarter of each year.

what is happening is not decreasing informality, but rather a new type of informality in the country from 1983 on. The evolution of the so-called urban informal sector at the beginning of the 1990s has a different dynamic from a decade ago. It is not increasing as a result of the expansion of small mercantile production, as in the past, but rather through the path of small capitalist production.

The question, however, does not end there. The dualist idea that the urban informal sector is a well-differentiated subsystem cannot explain the new forms of regulation that characterize the Chilean economy. It does not take into account the fact that the systematic implementation of neoliberalism in Chile, and the deregulation of markets that this implies, has fundamentally changed the nature of relations between capital and labor, as well as between sectors of capital and, above all, the type of economic regulation exercised by the state. Such a process makes it extremely complicated to understand manifestations of informality in the real world.

### Informal Sector or Informal Relations?

The use of the concept of the urban informal sector entails, now more than ever before, a number of theoretical and methodological problems.

First, informality cannot be simply defined as a group of activities necessary for survival, or just as a refuge for unemployed labor. As Portes, Castells, and Benton have remarked, it cannot be a "euphemism for poverty."[15] The so-called informal sector is a very heterogeneous category, in which the incomes of certain segments may be superior to those of the formal sector. This is certainly true in the Chilean case.[16]

Neither can informality be equated with the presence of a supposed precapitalist sector. The urban informal sector—whether in its narrower or wider definition—is certainly monetized. It may tend to operate on a "cash up-front" basis, but it also contains extensive circuits of informal credit, in Chile as around the world.[17]

Neither can informality be associated with the traditional, the non-modern, or the nonrational in the Weberian sense of the word. In fact, it represents a specific style of modernization, with a rationale different from that of the past.

Second, the boundaries of informality are not clear. The informal sector is made up not only of the self-employed but also of employers and waged workers who work in conditions that are not directly regulated by the state. Nevertheless, there are plenty of "formal" companies, operating as legal entities and paying taxes, that still operate with "informal" labor relations. They employ workers without legal contract, a widely prevailing practice in small and medium firms. This is particularly easy to do in Chile because labor legislation imposed in 1979 (and minimally modified in 1991) permits it, and the state plays a weak role in regulation of labor markets.

Large companies do not often resort to this type of practice. Nevertheless, adoption of a strategy that entails a reduction in the internal vertical integration of corporations, and hence an extensive reliance on subcontracting to small and medium companies, is widespread in Chile. This has two consequences. First, it establishes a new set of asymmetrical relations between large and small capital, involving agreements that relate not only to prices but to chains of distribution, direct credit, and the transfer of technology. These are organic relations that shape the market but are not regulated by the state. Second, subcontracting leads to new relations between labor and capital that are institutionalized neither by the state nor by collective negotiation, but rather by agreements between individual workers and employers. This increases the flexibility of capital and reduces the labor costs of the subcontracting company. Although such companies may be legally registered, the common practice is not to permit unions and to avoid collective bargaining. Their mixed employment practices, which include hiring workers with and without a contract, lead to precarious employment conditions for the work force.

As a result, a situation has arisen in Chile in which links in a chain of capital have appeared between what are traditionally understood as formal and informal companies. Formal companies, for example, use home workers in the clothes industry; and this format is repeated in various sectors of the economy (including the agro-export industry, mining, and forestry). Although such arrangements existed in the 1970s, they were without doubt far more widespread in the 1980s.

## The New Informality in Chile

In sum, then, a new process of informalization is under way, characterized by a change in the composition of the urban informal sector and by the informalization of an important segment of capital-labor relations, as well as of relations within capital. In this sense, it can be said that informality has increased, but in a very different manner from that suggested by the traditional use of the concept of informality.

Drawing on the preceding analysis, we can make four additional assertions with respect to the advance of informality in Chile. First, the mercantile form of informality (self-employed workers) did not increase, owing to the vigorous intervention of the authoritarian state in the labor market at times of deep economic crisis, using emergency work programs to provide the otherwise unemployed with waged work. These emergency programs first appeared between 1974 and 1975 and in 1982–83 employed more than half a million people. If that had not occurred, it is possible that an autonomous mercantile informal sector would have emerged, of a kind not linked to the formal sector. In this case, there could have been a dual economy.

Second, since the beginning of economic recovery in 1983, the recovery and expansion of small and medium firms has been accompanied by a new form of informality of a specifically capitalist nature. The urban informal sector of the 1990s is different from that at the beginning of the 1980s, especially because of the increased weight of waged workers.

Third, until the beginning of the 1980s, the informal and formal sectors in Chile were related predominantly through the survival strategies of poor families, who produced or sold wage goods or provided petty services. Currently, a productive relationship between the urban informal sector—in its widest sense—and the formal sector has emerged, based upon the kinds of production chains already mentioned. Rather than differentiated systems, therefore, there is a single complex system that is highly segmented. This is the case in numerous sectors of the Chilean economy and particularly those related to export.[18]

Fourth, informality is often associated with the disorganization of a matrix of institutional power—the profound crisis of an economic system and, in particular, a crisis of state regulation. In this sense, the urban informal sector can constitute a permanent escape from efforts made by a crisis-ridden state to reinforce or reinstate institutionalization.[19] This is not, however, the case in Chile. Informality in the 1990s is an integral part of a new matrix of power, not an escape from it, and reflects the effective reorganization of a political and economic system.

## Patterns of Change in the Services Sector

The growing importance of employment in the services sector of the Chilean economy was also a recurring theme in economic literature from the 1970s to the middle of the 1980s. Between 1960 and 1973,

FIGURE 4-4. *Employment in the Services Sector, 1970–94*

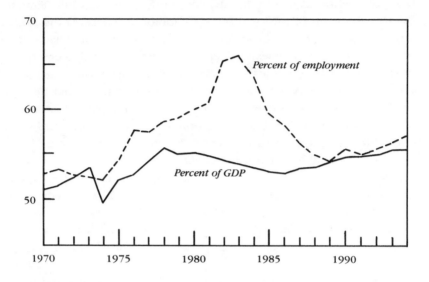

SOURCES: Central Bank of Chile; National Statistical Institute of Chile.

tertiary or service employment in Chile rose from 41 percent to 52 percent of total employment. The rate of growth became much more rapid
in the first decade of dictatorship, when employment in this sector rose
from 52 percent to 66 percent of total employment (see figure 4-4).[20]

Developments during the decade from 1973 to 1983 therefore appeared to reflect a structural tendency visible in the 1960s. Two arguments were put forward at the time to explain this phenomenon. The
first suggested that the growth of employment in the services sector
was a function of the growth of production within the industrial sector.
The second depicted this increasing service-sector employment as the
product of two processes: first, and of lesser overall importance, the
development of certain services typical of capitalist modernization
(such as financial services); second, and more important, the growth
of "spurious tertiarization," which involved hidden unemployment.[21]

The latter explanation seems most appropriate to describe the opening decade of the dictatorship. Given the stagnation and decline of
Chilean industry, one could speak of tertiarization with deindustrialization,[22] a process that took place not only during two recessions
(1974–75 and 1982–83) but also during a period of recovery (1976–

81 ). This pattern of capitalist development during 1973–83 was indicative of a growing autonomy of the services sector from the primary and secondary sectors. And, in spite of the fact that rapid development of finance and foreign commerce generated an expansion of employment, the relative weight of these in service-sector employment was very low.

In summary, the empirical evidence indicates that the principal source of employment in the tertiary sector at the time was of a "spurious" nature: it came from the expansion of small informal commerce, emergency work programs, and the growth of private services of various types that provided a refuge from the unemployment generated in other areas of the economy. This would appear to be the upshot both of a crisis in the old model of development (import-substituting industrialization) and the failure of the neoliberal export model.

## The End of the Old Form

During the 1980s the situation changed. In effect, during the economic recovery of 1984–90, the process of tertiarization was reversed. In those seven years, employment in the services sector fell from 64 percent to 51 percent of total employment.[23]

Statistics suggest that the current situation is not simply a reversal of the crisis of 1982–83, but indicates a change in employment behavior during economic recovery. This conclusion can be supported by comparing 1976–81 and 1983–88. In the first period, tertiary employment increased its relative weight in the work force from 52 percent to 57 percent, but in the second period that share fell from 64 percent to 51 percent.

Such a change in the pattern of employment in the services sector indicates modification of the dynamic of the economy as a whole and of the relations between sectors. Does this mean the end of tertiarization? There is not sufficient evidence to sustain this argument. As will be noted later, it would be more appropriate to talk of a new tertiarization, determined by new dynamics that lead to a change in the structure of the sector.

In fact, returning to the early debate over the nature of service-sector growth in Chile, the new evidence would suggest that if the idea of spurious tertiarization was correct for 1974 to 1983, the appropriate argument for the post-1989 period, once the decline of spurious tertiary employment was complete, could be very different: a period may have begun in which the growing importance of employment in the services sector is governed by the demand of the industrial sector for labor.

Whether this is in fact the case could be determined only by analyzing the course of change in the entire Chilean economy, which is well beyond the scope of this book. It is, nevertheless, important to move at this time beyond any analysis of the services sector as a single entity governed by certain similar economic "laws." The category takes in all those activities that are not classifiable in the primary and secondary sectors and whose only homogeneity lies in not producing material goods.[24] Furthermore, this sector—if it has ever existed as such—has a highly segmented dynamic and is moved by factors of very different types. A more detailed analysis of changes to the structure of tertiary employment would appear to bear this out.

## Disaggregating Service-Sector Employment

For the period from 1970 to 1990, four categories of service-sector employment can be identified: "spurious" employment, which includes emergency work programs and informal tertiary employment; public-sector employment; financial-sector employment; and tertiary employment linked to the dynamics of the primary and secondary sector and to the modern nonfinancial services sector.[25] The advantage of this classification is that it allows one to understand the very different factors that have influenced the course of change in each subsector while maintaining some continuity with the kinds of analysis put forward in the early 1980s.

DECLINE OF "SPURIOUS" TERTIARIZATION.    According to Aníbal Pinto, "spurious" tertiarization includes disguised unemployment and diverse forms of informal low-productivity activities.[26] To this must be added, in the Chilean case, the emergency work programs developed by the government between 1974 and 1986. The term "spurious" is synonymous with something deformed or bastardized and implies a process that deviates from the "normal." In this sense, the concept of spurious tertiary employment, although imaginative, is ambiguous and open to two possible interpretations. The first sees employment in low-productivity services as dysfunctional to an ideal-type economy, while the second sees it as a form of hypertrophy of "normal" historical tendencies—a phenomenon belonging to a period of crisis and transition from one regime of accumulation to another.

The first depiction is highly debatable. The repairmen, ice cream sellers, gas-fitters, and electricians, as well as the street vendors who hawk products manufactured in large- and medium-sized formal-sector companies, are all part of capitalist production and exchange. They are indispensable for assuring the material conditions of existence for high-, medium-, and low-income families. This being the case, there will always be a type of informal "low-productivity" employment that expresses visible and invisible, unstable, and precarious underemployment. It is not spurious by definition, and even less is it dysfunctional.

The second approach, linking spurious tertiarization to the hypertrophy of low-productivity employment in the services sector during a particular period of economic crisis and reorganization, predicts two possible outcomes. One is consolidation of the low-income tertiary sector as a phenomenon with its own dynamic and peculiar links with the rest of the economy. (This could have happened in Chile if the country had lived through a period of prolonged stagnation without the recovery and expansion that followed 1983.) The other is its reduction or even disappearance, as the crisis passes and it gradually stops functioning as a refuge for those sections of the labor force not absorbed by other sectors of the economy (including the rest of the services sector).

Statistical evidence for the Chilean case in 1984–88 suggests the latter outcome: spurious tertiary employment came to an end in Chile, at least until the next recession or prolonged structural adjustment. This does not mean the disappearance of all hidden unemployment or underemployment but rather the elimination of a kind of tertiary employment that operated as a haven for labor in a time of crisis and restructuring. It disappeared as the recovery of 1984–89 and the post-1989 expansion took hold.

An approach at estimating this phenomenon is the following. Let us calculate the level of informal employment in services plus population enrolled in emergency work programs as a percentage of the total labor force of Chile during 1970 and 1990. These years represent the extremes of the time period under consideration and can be considered normal years. The average of the figures for 1970 and 1990 is 11 percent, as can be seen in table 4-4, line 6.

Then let us calculate this same indicator during various other years between 1970 and 1990. As is shown in table 4-4, this series peaked at 25 percent in 1983. If spurious service-sector employment is defined as the difference between figures for various years in this series and the

TABLE 4-4. *Estimation of Spurious Service-Sector Employment,*
*Selected Years, 1970–90*

Thousands unless otherwise indicated

| Variable | 1970 | 1976 | 1980 | 1983 | 1986 | 1990 |
|---|---|---|---|---|---|---|
| (1) Labor force | 2,909 | 3,182 | 3,636 | 3,768 | 4,270 | 4,729 |
| (2) Population enrolled in emergency work programs | 0 | 158 | 191 | 503 | 221 | 0 |
| (3) Informal services employment | 321 | 359 | 485 | 433 | 481 | 546 |
| (4) 2 + 3 | 321 | 517 | 676 | 936 | 702 | 546 |
| (5) 4/1 (percent) | 11 | 16 | 19 | 25 | 16 | 12 |
| (6) 3/1 in normal years (1970 and 1990) (percent) | 11 | 11 | 11 | 11 | 11 | 11 |
| (7) 5 − 6 = spurious services employment (percent) | 0 | 5 | 8 | 14 | 5 | 1 |

SOURCE: National Statistical Institute of Chile (INE), National Employment Survey, fourth quarter of each year, with the exception of 1970, when figures refer to the third quarter.

average of 11 percent over the entire period, then it would seem (as indicated in line 7) that it rose to 14 percent in 1983, in the middle of the recession, and almost disappeared in 1990.

In sum, then, what can one conclude concerning the causes of the expansion and contraction of low-productivity, low-income tertiary employment in Chile between 1970 and 1990? The possible explanatory factors can be grouped in three categories: conjunctural, which stem from the economic cycle; long term, which stem from the rapid urbanization experienced by the country; and structural, related to the change in the regime of accumulation or economic development that shook the country during the first decade of the Pinochet dictatorship.

Turning first to the economic cycle, one would expect to see spurious tertiary employment consistently expanding and contracting in line with periods of recession and recovery. Although the low-income tertiary sector did contract during the 1984–90 recovery, nothing similar occurred during the earlier recovery of 1976–81. The vicissitudes of the economic cycle are thus not sufficient as an explanation of events.

The rhythm of metropolitan growth and urbanization does not provide a satisfactory explanation either. The available evidence indicates a decreasing tendency in the rate of urbanization between 1960 and 1990. The average annual rate of growth of the population in the metropolitan region fell from 3 percent to 2.3 percent between 1960–70 and 1980–90.

TABLE 4-5. *Employment in the Nonfinancial Public Administrative Sector, Selected Years, 1976–90*

| Type of employment | 1976 | 1980 | 1983 | 1986 | 1990 |
|---|---|---|---|---|---|
| Public employees (thousands) | 267 | 231 | 215 | 201 | 175 |
| Labor force (thousands) | 3,182 | 3,636 | 3,768 | 4,270 | 4,729 |
| Services employment (thousands) | 1,597 | 1,948 | 2,122 | 2,267 | 2,474 |
| Public employees/labor force (percent) | 8.4 | 6.4 | 5.7 | 4.7 | 3.7 |
| Public employees/services employment (percent) | 16.7 | 11.9 | 10.1 | 8.9 | 7.1 |

SOURCE: Government of Chile, Personnel Allotment, Budget Law.

To understand the evolution of spurious tertiary employment in Chile, then, it is necessary to look at the evolution of the concrete development strategy of the military government. During the latter 1970s unemployment in the public sector and in industry advanced rapidly, despite economic growth, while more than half a million workers came to have a precarious job in emergency programs, organized and badly paid by the state. In this way, the government managed to create a real "reserve army," which had by 1983 become even more important than the informal services sector, and which would rapidly disappear in the 1983–89 recovery. It is also necessary to look more carefully at other elements contributing to the evolution of tertiary employment—including spurious tertiary employment—between 1970 and 1990.

THE FALL IN PUBLIC EMPLOYMENT.   With the systematic implementation of neoliberalism, public employment fell progressively from 1973 on. Between 1972 and 1990, the proportion of the total work force accounted for by the public sector as a whole fell from 12 percent to 6 percent, a reduction from 360,000 to 280,000 employees.

If one looks only at the evolution of public employment in the tertiary sector (excluding employment in public companies that, privatized or not, constitute part of the secondary or primary sector), and if one furthermore excludes public employment in financial institutions, the picture is like that presented in table 4-5.

Tertiary public employment (nonfinancial) shows a persistent fall, in both absolute and relative terms. In absolute terms, the number of jobs declined 34 percent between 1976 and 1990. In relative terms, public employment in the tertiary sector fell from 8.4 percent to 3.7 percent

TABLE 4-6. *Employment in Financial Services, Selected Years, 1976–90*

| | Employment in financial services | | | |
|---|---|---|---|---|
| Year | Thousands | Percent of labor force | Percent of total employed | Percent of service-sector employment |
| 1976 | 63 | 2.0 | 2.3 | 3.9 |
| 1980 | 101 | 2.8 | 3.1 | 5.2 |
| 1983 | 110 | 2.9 | 3.4 | 5.2 |
| 1986 | 156 | 3.7 | 4.0 | 6.9 |
| 1990 | 203 | 4.3 | 4.6 | 8.2 |

SOURCE: National Employment Survey (INE), fourth quarter.

of the gainfully employed population. The importance of public employees in the services sector was reduced by slightly more than half.

As table 4-5 well illustrates, this was an almost linear process that did not depend on the ups and downs of the economic cycle, but rather on the will and capacity of the military government to apply a neoliberal project over a prolonged time period.

THE EXPANSION OF THE FINANCIAL SECTOR.    The growth of employment in the financial sector began in the middle of the 1970s—precisely at the time when financial capital began to develop its own dynamic, distinct from that of productive capital. The expansion of employment in the financial sector is due to the fact that the accumulation of capital took place at a faster rate than the increase in labor productivity in that sector.

During 1976–90, employment in financial services more than tripled (see table 4-6). From being a sector of marginal importance in tertiary employment, it came to take on a growing social significance, as witnessed by the fact that it eventually surpassed mining as a source of employment in Chile.

It should be noted that after 1983 the financial sector also diversified very quickly, leading to a fall in the relative weight of the banking sector. Between 1978 and 1990 the importance of the latter was reduced from 33 percent to 16 percent of all employment in the financial services sector.

PRODUCTIVE SERVICES AND THE NEW TERTIARIZATION.    Three subsectors can be grouped under the heading of productive services. The first contains those companies in the tertiary sector that depend upon the dynamics of growth and modernization in the agricultural and industrial sectors, such as service industries in the business of repair and maintenance, those involved in foreign trade, and transport companies. The second involves branches of modern commerce such as shopping centers, fast food restaurants, supermarkets, hotels, and tourism. This commercial subsector creates and sometimes controls long chains of economic activity that include sectors of transport and production, thus promoting change in production and processing technologies in many companies in the primary and secondary sector. The third is modern services such as the production of software and services that are eminently necessary for the reproduction of capital (such as advertising). The fate of this subsector depends not only on industry but also upon a general demand that arises within many spheres of the economy.

### The New Character of the Services Sector

Widening the analysis to take into account the last thirty years presents an interesting picture of the evolution of the tertiary sector in Chile. Several general conclusions can be drawn. First, during the 1960s there does not appear to have been a tertiarization of employment. Second, this process was concentrated in 1973–83, years characterized by two major recessions and a forced structural transformation. Third, the reversal of this process occurred during 1984–90, a period marked by the recovery and then the expansion (post-1988) of the Chilean economy.

The balance for 1984–94 would appear to show a process of "detertiarization" of employment. In reality, however, it might again be better to talk of a new type of tertiarization, of great importance in the economy, caused by an expansionary phase of capitalism and the consolidation of a new mode of capitalist regulation as well as a new form of organizing the economic system.

It is difficult to say whether the relative weight of services employment will continue to fall over the coming years. There are, however, some tendencies that can be predicted with a reasonable degree of certainty: public employment will not continue to fall, and it is probable that it will show a gradual recovery; financial employment will not grow further; and informal employment in services will become more stable, unless there is a new recession that could lead to a resurgence of spurious tertiary employment. Given these tendencies, and assuming that economic growth continues, the evolution of the tertiary sector will chiefly be determined by the development of productive services.

## The New Social Character of Poverty

The social character of poverty changed during the 1980s in Chile. At the beginning of that decade, poverty manifested itself in unemployment, in informal employment such as street vending, and in emergency work programs. By 1982, when almost a third of the labor force was openly unemployed, a consensus prevailed that anyone who did have work—especially in the formal sector, although wages there might be low—could be considered part of the middle-income stratum or a relatively privileged sector of the poor.

From the second half of the 1980s, in the heat of economic recovery, the employment situation began to improve. The same was not, however, the case for real wages. By 1990 the rate of unemployment had fallen to 5.7 percent, but average and minimum wages had not returned to their 1981 level and had grown further apart, indicating increasing wage differentiation.

### The Persistence of Inequality

The economic and occupational recovery of 1985–90 was centered around export growth and based upon low wages, a high level of internal oligopsony, and a flexible labor market with severe restrictions on unions. This recovery was accompanied, or perhaps consolidated, by a notable increase in social inequalities. Although data limitations make it difficult to document what took place during that crucial decade, information provided by the National Statistical Institute (INE) is extremely revealing. In 1978, the richest 10 percent of the population controlled 35 percent of all national income. Ten years later, the same decile received 42 percent. It is obvious that the situation of the poorest 40 percent had to get worse. In 1978, 14.5 percent of the national income went to this sector, while in 1988 the figure had fallen to 13.4 percent.

An evaluation of 1978–88 thus suggests a deterioration in the incomes of the poorest sectors. During this time, the official number of extremely poor rose from 12 percent to 15 percent of the national population, while the percentage of families officially considered to be poor rose from 24 percent to 26 percent. A pertinent indicator in this respect is the daily caloric consumption of the poorest 40 percent of the population, which fell 7 percent over the years under consideration. By 1990 the national household survey conducted by the new government found 5.2 million Chileans, or 40.1 percent of the total population, living in poverty.[27]

Since the installation of a democratic government in 1990, in circumstances of clear economic recovery, there has been a significant improvement in working conditions and wages. Between 1990 and 1992, the rate of unemployment fell from 5.7 percent to 4.7 percent, the lowest since 1971. At the same time, three developments have favored a progressive increase in workers' incomes. First, there has been a tightening in labor markets that has favored a gradual rise in wages, although not a fall in wage differentiation.[28] In this context, it is worth pointing out that there has also been an increase in hours worked per week, from an average of 48.5 in 1990 to 50.5 in 1992. Second, the number and membership of trade unions has grown. Between 1990 and 1992 union membership doubled, covering 22 percent of waged workers directly, but favoring indirectly around 35 percent, who received the benefits of collective negotiations and agreements. Third, the rate of inflation has fallen substantially from 27.3 percent in 1990 to 12.7 percent in 1992 and 8.2 percent in 1995. Given that wage adjustments are based on past inflation, this also favors a rise in workers' incomes.

Thus average real wages have grown at a moderate but sustained rate, outstripping their 1981 levels in 1992. As a result of this process, as well as the increase in social spending—which in Chile is effectively targeted toward low-income sectors—government estimates suggest that the number of people in poverty dropped from 5.2 million in 1981 to 4.5 million in 1992 and 3.8 million in 1994 (or 28 percent of the total population). In this case, 1.4 million people may have emerged from poverty by the end of the thirteen-year period.

Nevertheless, in spite of the increase in the real incomes of workers and of the poorest 40 percent of the population, there has been no significant change in the distribution of national and personal income. The share of national income attributable to wages fell between 1990 and 1992, and the richest 10 percent of all Chileans continues to receive around 40 percent of the total. There has not been any significant change in the distribution of national income by quintiles.

The figures just mentioned would suggest that while the number of people in Chile living in poverty is declining, the degree of inequality is not. How can one explain this apparent paradox?

One of the most obvious explanations is that average productivity has grown faster than average wages, which are earned by two-thirds of the employed. For the three-year period 1990–92, for example, the productivity-wage relation grew by 1.7 percent. Although not the subject of this book, there is therefore a clear need to analyze in greater detail the structural and institutional characteristics of the model of development that has continued to reproduce inequality—even though efforts are made to offset such a trend through an increase in social spending.

## Informality and Poverty

Official estimates for 1992 suggest that of the third of the labor force living in conditions of poverty, 20 percent live in rural areas, a proportion similar to the weight of these areas in the population as a whole. This means that the vast majority of the poor in Chile are to be found in urban areas.

Of the total poor in 1992, about 10 percent were unemployed. If one combines this group with another, composed of those who live in geographical areas that have been isolated or marginalized from the dynamic of growth (areas of structural decline), it appears that about a third of the total work force living in poverty could be described as "marginalized." This means that two-thirds of the labor force living in poverty cannot be explained by marginality. Such a situation constitutes one of the great changes with respect to the period from 1975 to 1983, when the vast majority of the poor were either unemployed or participating in emergency work programs.

New evidence from the household survey of 1990 (CASEN) reinforces the view that "informality" or marginality is no longer a good indicator of poverty in Chile. While those employed in formal occupations earn on average some 27 percent more than those in informal occupations, 45 percent of informal employment is located in the two highest income quintiles. Many jobs and professions in the informal sector are highly productive (and earn high incomes), and informality is not synonymous with backwardness or low productivity. Clearly, informality and poverty are not the same thing.

At the same time, many of those who are formally employed are poor. Forty-one percent of the two lowest income quintiles analyzed in the 1990 household survey are associated with formal urban employment, 25 percent are engaged in informal urban employment, and the rest are categorized under headings of agricultural employment or domestic service. This illustrates the fact that having a formal occupation does not necessarily imply escaping from poverty. Indeed, the ranks of the poor are made up to a great extent of people who would usually be considered formally employed.

### Precarious Waged Employment

Precarious waged employment constitutes the single most important element of poverty in present-day Chile. Such work may or may not be associated with some type of contractual arrangement. There is a sector of waged workers who do not have a formal contract and whose numbers are difficult to estimate. According to the CASEN survey, about 17 percent of the waged labor force in 1990 had no contract, while according to the Labor Studies Program (PET) the figure is around 30 percent. At any rate, it is clear that a significant minority of workers and staff have an informal wage situation, although this proportion shows a tendency to diminish over time. Simultaneously, however, a large proportion of those who do have a temporary or permanent contract are also subject to a precarious situation in their employment, encouraged by the current labor law, which allows a high level of flexibility in the use of the labor force by employers.

This precariousness is manifested in low levels of job stability, dependence upon income from piecework, poor working conditions, rigid specialization at work (which comes close to a neo-Taylorist form of organization), little access to training, few possibilities for internal mobility in the company, impediments to collective negotiation, low levels of participation and, sometimes, subjection to authoritarian relations in the workplace.

Precarious employment is not an anomaly of the market, nor does it derive from an atypical situation in certain small or traditional companies. The evidence from dozens of studies carried out in firms between 1988 and 1994 shows that precarious employment exists not only in small firms but also in the majority of medium firms and, to a certain extent, survives as well in large private companies.[29] Small companies, like the tens of thousands of small subcontracting firms that are now closely linked to more dynamic sectors of the Chilean economy, are not necessarily backward; and far from constituting a traditional or backward form of business behavior, precarious employment arises precisely from the style of capitalist modernization that has taken place in Chile over the past few decades.

As already noted, precarious employment is assured by labor legislation and by forms of official regulation of labor markets promoted by the dictatorship to ensure that firms could use labor flexibly. Recent reforms have not substantially modified the situation. At the same time, large companies have abandoned previous labor practices, which rested upon strategies to fix and stabilize the labor force, in favor of a flexible approach involving the subcontracting of many activities that were previously carried out within the company—particularly in large-scale mining and industry.[30] Furthermore, in the central valley, the traditional large landholding (*latifundio*) has been replaced over a number of decades by a multitude of medium and small agricultural producers subcontracted to large trading companies. In the South, the *latifundios* of the forestry sector that belong to large companies are not directly exploited by these companies but rather by subcontracted firms, and a similar situation prevails in the fishing industry.

In general terms, the large company controls a chain of small- and medium-sized subcontracted or supply companies of various types, which tend to situate themselves in small or medium urban centers at strategic points, ensuring economies of scale and access to good road transport.[31] Labor markets within the chain become sharply segmented. Workers who belong to the nucleus of the company, with stable employment, tend to be men who work full time, are permanent, and have a legal contract. Workers on the periphery, who have short-term contracts or work part time, are more often likely to be women. This is low-skilled work and there is an abundant supply of applicants in the labor market. Third, there are external workers who are hired by mining and forestry properties or by subcontracting companies.

Precarious employment rests upon an unstable and informal relation between labor and capital that varies according to the phase of the economic cycle and the degree of division of labor between companies. In the areas and sectors experiencing periods of expansion, with a consequent increase in the demand for labor, precarious employment does not necessarily decline in favor of more stable alternatives. Instead there is a change in the internal composition of precarious employment. The proportion of workers with sporadic employment, followed by unemployment, falls during certain times of the year, and the number of workers who can find employment throughout the year—in several jobs or through a number of temporary contracts—increases.[32] The individual is no longer limited to sporadic work in one company, but finds more regular work based on short-term contracts with various companies, or engages in different jobs (implying different working conditions) within the same company.

The situation in construction is very revealing in this respect. Employment in the sector is procyclical, but companies do not risk increasing the staff on a permanent contract when the economic picture improves. They have become accustomed to the advantages of flexibility provided by accumulated changes in the regulation of the labor market and processes of rationalization that began in the 1970s.[33]

A recent study draws attention to a similar tendency in the case of agriculture in the central valley, where a period of expansion and diversification of the productive structure implies attenuating the seasonal demand for labor. This means that even agricultural workers with temporary contracts must constantly shift jobs, and that the line between this work force and what is usually defined as occasional labor is very difficult to draw. In fact, the total number of agricultural laborers in Chile has probably been grossly overestimated, as a single person engaging in contract and occasional work might well have been counted several times. Employment surveys conducted by the National Statistical Institute would seem to confirm such fears, since seasonal differences for agricultural employment do not exceed 50,000, while claims are made for the existence of 400,000 temporary farm workers in Chile.[34]

In conclusion, then, poverty is no longer simply expressed in terms of unemployment and marginality, but is reproduced in new ways and among a wide stratum of workers. This places limits on strategies or policies for the redistribution of income that concentrate their efforts on the informal sector or the very small company. The conditions for equality cannot now be constructed through increased, focalized social expenditure. There is a growing need for the construction of more transparent and less distorted markets, more open and less authoritarian companies, greater access to education and training, more possibilities for union organization and participation at work, and wage and efficiency policies based on the just distribution of increases in productivity. All of these are decisive elements in any attempt to ensure a new treatment for labor, within a new context of development and democracy, in the small open economy of Chile.

# 5

# A Capitalist Revolution

Chilean history from 1964 to 1990 was profoundly traumatic for those who lived through the period. This is why consensus about the events that took place during this quarter of a century is so difficult. The government of Salvador Allende and the authoritarian regime of Augusto Pinochet will continue to divide future generations of intellectuals and politicians until the passage of time finally puts an end to these divisions.

Up to now, we have focused our attention principally on the period from 1973 to 1990. The two milestones of this era were the military coup of 1973 and the start of the democratic transition during 1988–90—both events that had an enormous impact on the Chilean nation. Reference to this period, however, reflects contingent approaches that criticize or eulogize the old authoritarian regime and do not recognize any continuity between the years before and after 1973. The year 1973 marks a deep rupture that is positive for some and tragic for others. In this approach, the period before 1973 appears almost as a pre-history, a shattered past that entered into irreversible crisis and today appears to be buried forever. It is worthwhile, nevertheless, to take a different approach.

In our opinion, although 1973 symbolizes the crisis and rupture of an era, it is also part of a much larger process of change encompassing approximately a quarter of a century. Put simply, between 1964 and 1990 Chile lived through a period of transformation that altered its historical foundations. The governments of Frei (1964–70), Allende (1970–73), and Pinochet (1973–90) attempted, in different ways and with different orientations, to carry out projects for the radical trans-formation of the country. In this sense, they were all revolutionary governments with a highly ideological base, dominated by elites with a far-reaching sense of purpose, whose diagnosis was of a crisis in society, the economy, and the political system, requiring radical change.

It is clear that what took place in this quarter of a century was *not at all* a group effort carried out by three successive governments. The military government cut short and reversed what had been started under Frei and Allende. The final and definitive direction was imposed by the military regime, which carried out great structural transformations, especially in the economic sphere. This gave rise to the term "neoliberal revolution." But although the destruction of what had gone before was profound and extensive, what took place between 1973 and 1990 was also based partly on the transformations that had been carried out by preceding governments.

To a large extent, the radical nature of the neoliberal project was possible because the attempts that had preceded it were also radical. Given the dimension of the changes that took place, it would seem appropriate to speak of a revolutionary epoch, which was not confined to the political sphere but covered the society and economy as well. Rather than a neoliberal revolution, it would be better to speak of a capitalist revolution, with a radical transformation of the regime of accumulation and the mode of regulation in the most fundamental aspects of the economic system, including the state, the firm, markets, wages, and private property. A simple focus on neoliberalism does not permit full understanding of this process.

## The Neoliberal Reorientation of Previous Reforms

The paradox of the events that took place between 1964 and 1990 is that the forces that sought to impose their goals were diametrically opposed and acted in the name of very different principles from what actually came to pass. The Christian Democrats and Popular Unity did not envisage liberalizing the capitalist order but rather reforming or eliminating it. They did not seek to weaken the state but to reform it and strengthen it. Their actions, however, eventually facilitated the task of the military regime. There are three striking examples of this point.

### Nationalization and Privatization

The Frei government carried out a program of industrialization based largely on public investment, which increased the power of the state. In addition, steps were taken to strengthen national control over natural resources through the so-called Chileanization of copper. The Allende government accelerated this process, nationalizing copper and the entire mining and banking industry. There were also interventions in, and confiscations of, large properties in the industrial and agricultural sectors belonging to economic groups, both old and new. In spite of the differences between the two governments, there was continuity in the sense that an enormous amount of power and wealth was concentrated in the hands of the state.

With the advent of military rule, a prolonged process of privatization and reprivatization began, which involved more than 500 public companies and developed in two great waves. The last of these privatizing drives took place in the period from 1985 to 1990 and included service companies that had been in the hands of the state since the 1930s. This allowed for the extension of private accumulation into areas that had hitherto been out of bounds. In fact, privatization can be understood as a process of primary accumulation, insofar as the prices of public companies were set below their (theoretically estimated) market value. The sale of state enterprises facilitated the emergence of new economic groups, some of technocratic origin, as well as the entrance of foreign capital in areas that had been restricted due to the pressure of domestic private capital. In general terms, the assets of the state became capital, and the waged work of public company employees became productive. Public investment during 1938–73 was transformed into a stock of private capital that, to be fully utilized, had to be subject to an intense and rapid process of rationalization.

This means that the buildup of public companies in the period from 1938 to 1973 and the nationalizations of the period from 1970 to 1973 were the prelude to an expansion of capitalism toward the state. Something similar, but on a much larger scale, is now taking place in the countries of eastern Europe. Ironically, it could be said that the nationalizing state was reexpropriated in the 1970s and 1980s. Far from representing a return to the past, privatization served as a new source of capitalist accumulation and as the basis for the reconstruction of a new business class.

### The State and the Nationalization of Copper

It is striking that copper escaped the great privatizing drive of the military regime. It would seem that, in this instance, pragmatism triumphed over ideology, because there were always pressures for privatization. Nevertheless, this pragmatism concealed a far more basic fact. Capitalism has never existed without a state. The market economy has never functioned well without a strong state. Furthermore, it was impossible to carry out a neoliberal transformation without a strong state that could overcome a serious fiscal crisis.

The nationalization by the Allende government of large-scale copper mining, which until 1971 had been in the hands of transnationals, as well as the founding of CODELCO, significantly increased state income in both foreign and domestic currency. During the neoliberal period between 1974 and 1989, this export sector generated additional resources of móre than U.S. $10 billion, which had a very positive effect on the balance of payments and the budget. Particularly with the increase in the price of copper after 1985, the state could count on enormous resources, which allowed it to avoid a prolonged fiscal crisis, rescue the financial sector, and gradually address the crisis of external debt.

## Agrarian Reform and the Land Market

The agrarian reform implemented between 1964 and 1973 destroyed the old agrarian order in Chile without creating a new one, in contrast to the experience of Mexico (with the *ejido*), the USSR (with the *kolkhoz* and *sovkhoz*), or Yugoslavia (with the self-governing cooperative). But it was precisely the weakening of the landowning oligarchy that, after 1973, allowed the military government to assert its autonomy from the forces of the old oligarchical order while simultaneously unleashing fierce repression against the peasant movement—perhaps the cruelest and most extensive repression in Chile's modern history.

With the demobilization of both the peasantry and the landowning oligarchy, the military government began a process of partial return of expropriated lands, accompanied by the allocation of land titles to smallholders who, given their lack of credit and technical assistance, were quickly forced to sell. The pattern of sales of agricultural properties between 1973 and 1979 completely changed the nature of the agrarian sector.

A market in land was created that had previously not existed, and a new business class appeared, which reorganized the old agricultural structure based around the *latifundio* and replaced the labor practices associated with it. Thus an ideal climate was created for the advance of capitalism in the Chilean countryside once the old patterns of pre-capitalist development had been broken.

The importance for neoliberal reform of measures taken by Christian Democrats and the Popular Unity government can be explored through considering three negative propositions:

First, if the Allende government had not nationalized a significant number of firms, the process of centralization of capital would in all probability have been halted by the resistance of the business sector, which would have applied pressure for the maintenance of a protective and developmentalist state. And if publicly owned assets had not been available for privatization, a major element in the process of neoliberal accumulation would have been missing. The nominal depreciation of physical capital was possible only through the sale of state-owned enterprises at low prices. The degree of capital mobility that came about—including a breathtaking degree of movement on the part of domestic and foreign economic groups after 1985—depended upon privatization.

Second, if copper had not been previously nationalized, it is difficult to imagine that the military government—which was urgently seeking to cultivate good relations with the United States and to create conditions of security for foreign investors—would have expropriated important transnational firms. Without the revenue generated by copper, the fiscal crisis would have continued, and prospects for the recovery of the financial system—and of the Chilean economy—would have been much weaker.

Third, if a drastic and extensive agrarian reform had not been carried out before the coup, this necessary task would in all likelihood have been postponed, as it was in Brazil. The Pinochet government (acting in the defense of private property) certainly would not have confronted the landowning oligarchy. Because of the weak position in which the prior agrarian reform had left the oligarchy, however, the military regime enjoyed considerable room for maneuver. If the agrarian reform had not previously taken place, the most likely scenario would have been the modernization of the *latifundio*. This would have occurred on a much more limited scale than proved to be the case in the 1980s and could not have generated the competitive capacity shown by the current system, which is based on the small and medium agricultural enterprise, linked through subcontracting to agro-industry and the export market.

These speculations allow us to put forward the following argument: between 1964 and 1973, the governments of Eduardo Frei and Salvador Allende not only dissolved what was left of the old oligarchical order but also began to dismantle the foundations of the particular capitalist order that had been constructed since the 1930s and had been showing signs of crisis since the 1950s. During this period, new social movements emerged—youth, peasants, and shantytown dwellers—who questioned the old social order and modified the logic of programs for social change. Still more decisively, during this period, the ruling classes saw their power gravely weakened and had to contemplate the possibility that only radical social change would permit a reconstitution of their leadership. This led to a revolutionary situation in the strictest Leninist sense: neither those at the top nor those at the bottom could continue in the same way as before.

Later, between 1973 and 1989, Chile lived under a dictatorship that operated on the assumption that the country was at war. The military regime tried to mold all areas of the social landscape to conform to principles of possessive individualism, patriarchal authoritarianism, and the total separation of the public from the private. Subsequent history showed that it did not succeed completely in this objective, but it still managed to produce transformations of an extraordinary magnitude. There was a capitalist reorientation of agrarian reform and the creation of a market in land, the financial system was liberalized and a capital market established, the economy was opened to the exterior and transnationals, and the firm was rationalized and subject to authoritarian modernization.

The task of neoliberalism was made considerably easier by the radical nature of the reforms carried out by the two previous governments. This is not to undervalue the audacity of the military and the neoliberal technocrats, but it explains the context in which their so-called modernizations could be almost completely realized. This seems to us to be a characteristic of the Chilean experience that is of fundamental importance for comparative studies. It indicates that the opportunities for a successful and radical capitalist transformation are better in those societies that have experienced a previous process of advanced socialization.

There is another important aspect that must be taken into account. Those who began the revolution did so by attacking the old order, a mixture of oligarchical and capitalist structures only partially integrated into world markets and protected by the state. But they did not succeed in articulating a new order. At the time of the military coup, both society and economy were in transition; new structures had not crystallized, but were in flux—a kind of liquid state, in which they were susceptible to transformation and new directions. Thus, although they neither expected nor desired to do so, the elites who supported Frei and Allende paved the way for Pinochet and his civilian technocrats to modify their original objectives in favor of a program of systematic, radical reforms of a neoliberal type.

## The Role of the Elites: From Revolution to Moderation

A blueprint for the process of change that occurred in Chile between 1964 and 1990 could not be found in any manual or theoretical text. The "revolution" was not imposed from the outside, nor was it an endogenous process that can be attributed to market forces. It was the result of transformations undertaken by three foundational governments, although its definitive profile was constructed under the military government.

What took place between 1964 and 1990 is quite astonishing in its profundity. There is no similar experience in twentieth-century Chile. The only parallel can be found between 1860 and 1880, a period of crisis involving enormous territorial expansion toward the south, during the wars associated with the last Mapuche rebellions, and toward the north, with the occupation of 180,000 square kilometers of land in the wars with Peru and Bolivia. In contrast to that earlier experience, the recent expansion of Chilean capitalism has not been territorial, although it has certainly implied extensive growth toward new areas of accumulation. There are similarities between the periods from 1860 to 1880 and from 1964 to 1990. In both cases, the decisive and bloody battles were undertaken by the military. In contrast to the last century, however, in modern times the changes were initiated by civilians from the left and center, to be quickly appropriated by the ruling classes in order to conquer state and social areas or, in other words, markets and sources of accumulation.

Although the scope of these changes invites use of the term "revolution," at no time was it a "silent revolution,"[1] which would imply that it was brought about by the inexorable advance of civil society or market forces. The Chile of 1990 was not created by a process of capitalist expansion that inevitably dismantled the foundations of the old order. On the contrary, the rate of growth between 1964 and 1990 was well below the levels achieved in other countries that also experienced similar periods of radical transformation, such as the United States (1880–1910), Brazil (1960–80), and South Korea (1960–90). What occurred was a revolution imposed from above, from the upper ranks of the state, which during 1964–90 was governed successively by three political elites, all with programs for the radical transformation of the country.

The origins of this historical process can be found in the 1950s, when the first version of neoliberalism appeared with the Klein-Sachs mission (a technical consultancy, contracted by the Ibáñez government in its bid to bring down inflation), while the left set out a program of advanced structural change and the Christian Democrat party was formed. From then on, and throughout 1958–89, all governing elites were revolutionaries, although in distinct times and situations. The "revolution in liberty," the "peaceful road to socialism," and the "neoliberal revolution" were all radical programs of systemic change.

The struggle between the elites was implacable. Once in government or power, each faction argued for the necessity of overcoming the burdens of the past. During the rule of the center and the left, both agreed on the need to sweep away the remnants of the old oligarchical order but differed as to whether it was necessary to reform or overcome capitalism. The right, after abandoning its useless efforts to return to the past, came to understand the gains to be made from capitalist modernity and decided upon a radical and global transformation of economy, society, and even the state, whose business and protectionist features they had helped to build up over half a century. Over this entire period, therefore, the discourse of the governing elites always appealed to modernity and structural transformation, although with very diverse and opposing meanings.

Nevertheless, when each elite was in opposition, exactly the opposite took place. At first, it was the right, in the name of preserving the old order, which violently attacked the Christian Democrat and Popular Unity governments. But after the military coup, the neoliberal revolution was severely criticized by the Christian Democrats and the left, which also appealed to the past and to the traditional order, idealizing to a certain degree the old-style, crisis-ridden capitalism and forgetting the implacable criticisms they had made of it during the 1950s.

Thus all the elites—when not in power—defended the old order, in which their supporters appeared to have lived better, and emphasized the destruction, disorder, anomie, and insecurity caused by the process of modernization. All the elites denounced the omnipotence of the state; the right spoke of totalitarianism, while the center and the left spoke of authoritarianism and dictatorship. And with these discourses they succeeded in undermining the governing faction.

These were not just the vagaries of politics. The elites did not act alone amidst a sea of social tranquillity. They were interpreting a vast range of social interests. They loosened the chains that restricted the constitution and mobilization of classes, groups, actors, and social movements. Thus, in successive stages, the whole of Chilean society was mobilized and thrown into a whirlwind of transformation. Great movements shook the country and the three elites were carried on the crests of these waves. Not even the repression that followed the coup of 1973 could prevent, a decade later, the reappearance of the oppressed masses, although it was only for a short period (1983–86) in an attempt to remodel society and reconstitute a political system that seemed to have disappeared under the boots of the military.

In this process, all the elites who initiated this succession of radical changes ended up by losing political power. The Christian Democrats were overtaken by the left and the right, while Popular Unity was overthrown in its third year of government. *Pinochetismo*, which, in contrast to its predecessors, managed to complete its program of economic and political changes, was also defeated—thus in the end obtaining only a pyrrhic victory, as has often occurred in history. But the successive and combined action of these three forces produced a capitalist revolution, confirmed by the nature of the order constituted and the class that it strengthened.

## Structures, Movements, and Social Actors

Although elite groups appear to have played the principal role in the transformations that took place over the last thirty years, it is clear that history is much more complex than this, since the elites have also been overtaken by historical events. The wider the historical perspective adopted, the more this fact becomes apparent. What was the relationship between these structural changes and changes in the area of social action? The argument of this study is that the history of social movements between 1972 and 1992 can be understood only in relation to the profound changes that took place in the social structure.

By way of an example, we can consider resistance to the dictatorship. This might have been very different without the changes in industrial employment that took place in the 1960s. Yet the drastic reduction in industrial employment between 1975 and 1980 shows that the defeat of the workers' movement was not achieved through repression alone. Neoliberal reform and structural adjustment destroyed the social bases that had nourished the power of unions and left-wing parties in the 1960s. Equally, the history of the protests might have been very different if the economic crisis had lasted. This would have led to continuing unemployment and informality, conditions that produced many of the protagonists of the protests. Again, events were different, as economic recovery changed the social structure and weakened the social and cultural bases that had supported the great mobilizations between 1983 and 1986.

It is possible to interpret what took place between 1973 and 1993 in terms of three cycles that affected the social circumstances of both popular and middle sectors. In the first cycle, there was an alteration of the social structure that emerged from import substitution and the social contract in Chile and lasted for almost half a century, from the 1930s to the mid-1970s. The most important features of this period were rapid urbanization concentrated in the metropolitan region, a growth in waged work, and an increase in industrial and public employment. It was a period in which big private and public companies, with a high use of labor, employed a predominantly male labor force. This was stable employment with collective contracts, influence over the organization of production, and a significant presence of political parties.

The exhaustion of this phase came after the military coup of 1973, deepening after 1975 and ending in collapse during the crisis of 1982–83. A dramatic opening of national markets to foreign competition, stagnation of the real exchange rate, two deep recessions (1975–76 and 1982–83), and the deregulation of labor markets brought rapid change. Firms were drastically rationalized, leading to high unemployment but also allowing companies to regain control over the production process and to use labor flexibly. At the same time, privatization caused a reduction in public employment.

The second cycle was linked to the rise and decline of social relations produced by these neoliberal reforms. By 1982 more than half of the labor force (53.3 percent) was either unemployed, in emergency work programs, or in the informal sector. Large numbers of young people and the unemployed were concentrated in low-income settlements, leading to two simultaneous and related processes. The first was a social anomie of the type described by Durkheim. The second was the appearance of new networks of solidarity of a territorial nature (shantytown, neighborhood, street), supported by the church, nongovernmental organizations, and political parties. Both processes must be understood in order to make sense of the protests of 1983 and the complex social phenomena underlying them.

This structure of interaction developed between 1973 and 1983, but began to decline after 1984. Almost ten years after the crisis of 1983, the percentage of workers who were unemployed or part of the informal sector had fallen to 29.5 percent. Between 1983 and 1993, more than a million workers found employment, which led to a dissolution of the social structures that had formed during the period from 1973 to 1983.

The third cycle is associated with new patterns of social relations emerging from export-led development. The period from 1983 to 1993 was completely different from the preceding decade; waged work grew, informal employment fell, and even absolute poverty fell. There was a striking increase in industrial employment, which grew from less than 350,000 in 1982 to nearly 840,000 in 1993. But labor relations and welfare provisions bore little resemblance to those of the pre-1973 period.

There have been corresponding changes in the organization of civil society. The anomie and solidarity networks that were produced during the period of neoliberal adjustment have been altered. There is now more emphasis on the workplace than the neighborhood. Between 1982 and 1992, the number of unions grew from 4,048 to 10,725, and the number of members increased from 347,000 to 723,000. A new process of formation of collective identities can be seen, although at the same time other values and identities are being lost.

In sum, social movements developed within three distinct situations. The first was the dismantling of the structures that had emerged over four decades until 1973. The second was the emergence of social movements linked to the days of protest between 1983 and 1986. The principal actors in these protests were not the workers, as was the case in Brazil in 1979, but residents of low-income settlements and unemployed youth. This was a transitory phenomenon, although some thought at the time that it might become more permanent. After 1986, with the decline of the protests and their transformation into a civil movement directed by a coalition of democratic parties, a new process began. This was manifested in the slow but sustained growth of social organizations such as unions and official neighborhood committees, reflecting not only the gradual appearance of new opportunities, but also the constitution of a new social structure that was more organic than its immediate predecessor. Because of the open nature of the Chilean economy, however, this structure was also unstable.

## The 1990s: Waiting for the New Actors

The study of the behavior of social actors during the decade of 1983–93 raises many questions, not all of which have been adequately answered. There is a striking contrast between 1983 and 1993. In the first year, a wave of protests, and the social movements which they engendered, marked a turning point in Chilean society. They appeared very rapidly, considering that during the previous decade opposition to the military regime had been weak and dispersed. Nevertheless, contrary to expectations, the protests and social movements did not continue to grow. They entered a period of decline and after 1986 were absorbed into a vast civic movement centered upon the political parties that triumphed in the 1988 plebiscite. In the mid-1990s, there is a new range of social actors who have little in common with their predecessors: they are less militant and not so disposed to adopt conflictual positions. The predictions of the majority of observers—whether hopeful or catastrophic—have not come to pass.

Within the context of a democratic transition, in which the economy is growing but vast social inequalities continue to exist, there has not been an explosion of social conflict but an atmosphere of relative social calm. This contrasts with the experiences of Brazil, Argentina, and Uruguay. Moreover, since 1988, the radical libertarian and antisystemic views present during 1983–86 have been swept away by a tide of cultural conservatism and political realism. The action of the political elites has been transformed into the art of the possible, putting a brake for some years on the development of new social projects. So-called new social movements have not emerged; instead there has been a recovery in the union movement, operating on a pragmatic basis but with a capacity that could not have been expected twenty years ago.

Our generation has seen an exceptional period of transformation, marked by social and political struggle among elites with radical projects for the transformation of society. The winner of one of these battles is well known. But the subsequent transformations are extraordinarily complex. The social movements that emerged and then disappeared in the 1980s would appear to belong to a past era. The new ones still speak haltingly, in a different language. Over time, they will renew a country still marked by twenty years of oppression and will strengthen civil society in a multitude of new ways.

# Notes

## Introduction

1. Mario Góngora, *Ensayo histórico sobre la noción de estado en Chile en los siglos XIX y XX* (Santiago: Ediciones La Ciudad, 1981).

## Chapter 1

1. "Representative bodies" of the state are those directly or indirectly renewed through elections (parliament, the presidency, and other high administrative positions filled through political appointment). "Permanent bodies," on the other hand, are professional institutions, formally independent of the popular will as expressed through elections (the judiciary, the armed forces, the stable personnel of public administration).

2. On "ibañismo" and the second government of Carlos Ibáñez, see the study by Jean Bernadette Brugel, "Populism, Nationalism and Liberalism in Chile: The Second Administration of Carlos Ibáñez, 1952–1958," Ph.D. thesis, University of Liverpool, 1986. On the government of Eduardo Frei and the Christian Democrats, see the study by Ricardo Yocelevsky, *La Democracia Cristian chilena y el gobierno de Eduardo Frei* (Mexico: El Colegio de México, 1989).

3. A dramatic and detailed account of the events, illustrating this collapse of the possibilities for representative politics, can be found in the posthumous book by the then commander-in-chief of the army, General Carlos Prats González, *Testimonio de un soldado* (Santiago: Pehuén, 1985).

4. On this same point, see chapter 3.

5. The title of captain-general was assumed by General Pinochet and created expressly for him.

6. *The Prince*, chap. 5.

7. This calculation is based on the input-output matrix for the Chilean economy in 1977. On the usefulness of this indicator as a measure of power, see Fernando Cortés and Ana Jaramillo, "Relaciones de poder en los conflictos laborales," El Colegio de Mexico, Mexico City, 1979.

8. On these figures and the concept of the "inorganic" in the employment structure, see Javier Martínez and Eugenio Tironi, *Las clases sociales en Chile: Cambio y estratificación, 1970–1980* (Santiago: SUR, 1983).

9.  See Carlos Hunneus, *Los chilenos y la política: Cambio y continuidad en el autoritarismo* (Santiago: CERC-ICHEH, 1987), p. 34.

10. *Trattato di sociologia generale* (Florence: Barbera, 1916).

11. A definitive and exhaustive example of its criticisms of the revolutionary road can be found in the Central Committee document, *El ultra-izquierdismo, Caballo de Troya del Imperialismo* (1975).

## Chapter 2

1. To have a better idea of the differences between Mexico and Chile, one can look at the geography of their international trade. Mexico is an open country, bordered to the south by a group of small Central American countries that account for only 0.7 percent of its foreign trade. To the north, it has a vast frontier with the United States, the largest economic force in the world, which represents 65 percent of Mexico's foreign trade. Not only goods and capital but millions of people travel across this border. By contrast, Chile is a thin and isolated country, hemmed in by the Pacific, the Andes, the Atacama desert, and Antarctica. Only 3.1 of its exports and 8.1 percent of its imports are carried out with neighboring countries (Argentina, Peru, and Bolivia), while the United States represents only 21 percent of its foreign trade. Fifty-six percent of this trade takes place with Europe and Japan. A free trade agreement with the United States therefore will not have the same impact as it will for Mexico: the bigger impact will arise from Chile's integration into MERCOSUR.

2. Until now, only the Mexican experience compares with the Chilean. In Mexico, of the 1,155 industries controlled by the state in 1982, only 223 remained by May 1992. In both countries the privatization process is virtually complete, although it is striking that both PEMEX (petroleum) and CODELCO (copper) have remained outside the privatization programs.

3. During Popular Unity (1970–73), not only were a large number of firms nationalized, but an even larger number were under government administration, although not legally removed from their owners. Furthermore, there was a large sector of industrial and agrarian properties that had been taken over briefly by workers with the aim of securing government intervention.

4. In ninety-one of these companies it had a majority share. CORFO also transferred to the private sector its shareholdings in sixteen commercial banks. At the same time, more than 600 sales of mining assets, agro-industrial plants, and property took place.

5. Through these methods, different parts of the "grey area" (companies in which the state had intervened) were transferred to the private sector. Big industrial firms and their subsidiaries were controlled by new local economic groups, transnational corporations, and a combination of both. Foreign investors concentrated on the social security companies (AFP) and the insurance market, which were controlled by North American finance groups such as Bankers Trust, Aetna, and American International Group. Among them, these groups controlled 65 percent of the shares of the AFP. The reprivatization of the large banks that had been taken over during the

crisis followed a different path. The new owners were not national economic groups or foreign companies but rather the technocrats responsible for their administration, who were now converted into bankers.

6. Mario Marcel, *La privatización de las empresas públicas en Chile* (Santiago: CIEPLAN, 1989).

7. The most dramatic crisis was that involving the finance company La Familia, which belonged to members of the government. After making loans to its owners, it was declared bankrupt. The government covered deposits, but only partially.

8. Between 1974 and 1981, the number of banks doubled from twenty-one to forty-five. At the same time, while the savings and loan associations were moving toward extinction, financial companies, which had not existed at all before 1974, numbered twenty-one in 1981. The share of private banks in the financial system rose from 45 percent to 70 percent, while that of the state bank fell from 35 percent to 15 percent. Along with diversification, there was also a high level of concentration. Five banks controlled 60 percent of banking credit, 64 percent of other financial credit, and 30 percent of the foreign debt in 1981.

9. Medium and long-term debt—that is, debt not controlled by the IMF—rose from $3.261 billion in 1973 to $12.5 billion in 1978.

10. Eight percent of the agricultural holdings in Chile, with an area of more than 200 hectares each, controlled 90 percent of the arable land of the country in 1960. At the same time, there were 46,000 properties of less than 1 hectare and 160,000 properties of less than 10 hectares. Together these accounted for 60 percent of all farms. Change in this extremely polarized agrarian sector was stymied from 1938 on, when the parties of the right adhered to a plan for industrialization in exchange for a commitment not to reform agricultural property or to permit peasant unionization. The dominant model of industrialization in Chile led to the transfer of surpluses—through price differentials—from the agricultural to the industrial sector.

11. The number of beneficiary families reached 61,000, to which should be added 15,000 single men who had previously been landless tenants. Landholdings with over 80 hectares of "basic irrigation-quality" land were expropriated, leaving the owners with a reserve or concession. However, given the number of peasants demanding land, this was insufficient; and a proposal was made to expropriate holdings over 40 hectares, without leaving a reserve. Peasants were grouped into settlements or cooperatives.

12. See "Copper Revenue during the Military Regime," *Colección Estudios CIEPLAN*, no. 24 (1988), pp. 85–111. The estimates for 1989 are by Alvaro Díaz.

13. Until 1983 the government imposed automatic wage adjustments. More recently, coercive regulation has operated through the labor plan. Minimum salaries have been readjusted on a staggered basis, so that between 1981 and 1989 they fell behind average salaries.

14. For two decades, an attempt has been made to develop an appropriate theoretical approach for exploring the simultaneous nature of coordination through markets and coordination through private or public hierarchies. This new perspective deviates from the principal current of economics and,

without rejecting the necessary rigor of the discipline, actively seeks a new alliance with other areas of social science such as history, political science, and sociology in order to escape from the limits and restrictions imposed by positivist theory. Especially important in this development have been the works of the economic historian Alfred Chandler; Oliver Williamson, who laid the basis for a neo-institutional approach to transaction costs; and Alfred Eichner, who developed a post-Keynesian analysis of the new microeconomy as the basis for an exploration of new macroeconomic approaches.

15. Ronald H. Coase, "The Nature of the Firm," *Economica*, vol. 4, n.s. 386 (1937), pp. 386–405.

16. Taylorism is the method of scientific organization of labor pioneered by Frederick Winslow Taylor (1856–1915), who developed a set of studies to rationalize production, perfect the division of labor, and increase productivity through time-saving devices. Among his most famous works is *The Principles of Scientific Management* (New York: Harper and Brothers, 1911).

17. Alain Lipietz and Danielle Leborgne, "El Fordismo y su espacio," *Revista de Ciencias Económicas* 1–2 (San José, Costa Rica, 1988).

18. Barbara Garson, *The Electronic Sweatshop* (Penguin Books, 1988).

## Chapter 3

1. This was facilitated by old legislation that had fallen into disuse and had been established in the critical days of the "Socialist Republic" of 1931. The law allowed the designation of administrators in the case of an obvious boycott on the part of the firm's directors.

2. Guillermo Campero, *Los gremios empresariales en el período 1970–1983: Comportamiento sociopolítico y orientaciones ideológicas* (Santiago: Instituto Latinoamericano de Estudios Transnacionales, 1984), p. 58. With respect to this period, as well as the first ten years of military government, we refer the reader to this study by Campero, which provides much of the information for this chapter.

3. Ibid., p. 290.

4. Ibid.

5. Ibid.

6. Ibid. For many *gremio* members from this sector, the aspiration was to integrate the movement with the state, as was proposed in the "multi-gremial congress" that took place at the beginning of December 1973. The principal idea was to create councils at the regional and local level to resolve socioeconomic questions. These would be made up of representatives of the military government and civic multi-gremial councils. See Campero, *Los gremios empresariales*; the complete resolutions can be found in "Actas Congreso Multigremial," *El Mercurio* (Santiago), December 12, 1973.

7. Tomás Moulián and Pilar Vergara, *Estado, ideología y políticas económicas en Chile, 1973–1978* (Santiago: CIEPLAN, 1979).

8. Juan Gabriel Valdés, *La Escuela de Chicago: Operación Chile* (Buenos Aires: Grupo Editorial Zeta, 1989), p. 17.

9. "Constitutionally," if this word can be used, this would have been the appropriate succession. With the president of the republic dead and his

ministers incapacitated, the constitution determined that the presidency should go to the president of the Senate. At the time, this was the ex-president of the republic and leader of the Christian Democrats, Eduardo Frei Montalva. It was the hope that this would take place that led many leaders of the Christian Democrats to support the coup and the military junta.

10. This ideology is based on the political thought of the famous statesman Diego Portales (1793–1837), probably one of the most important political thinkers during the era of state building in Latin America. Among the many characteristics of his political personality was his independence from the multiple parties and political factions of the time. This conviction, combined with his authoritarian approach to power, has been emphasized by historians (a principal source for the formation of the military mentality) and was always linked to the "foundational" nature of his work. Portales created a formal state that gave political continuity to the republic for nearly half a century, while neighboring countries were submerged in repeated struggles for power.

11. For this group, it was not a case of returning to the pre-Allende development path but rather, in the words of their intellectual leader, Sergio de Castro, of reversing "three previous decades of failed policies," given that "the results of the previous government [Popular Unity] were only the culmination of a previous tendency."

12. Rolf Luders in Pedro Ibáñez Ojeda and Rolf Luders, "Una economía para Chile," mimeo, Santiago, June 1983, cited in Valdés, *La Escuela de Chicago*, p. 16.

13. The convergence between a military elite and an educational elite was not without precedent in the contemporary history of Chile. The period of civil peace and institutional stability that began in the 1930s and collapsed at the beginning of the 1970s, and was based on a strategy of import-substituting industrialization, originated from a similar alliance between the military and civil engineers. The difference this time was the personalization of military power.

14. Harry G. Johnson, *On Economics and Society* (University of Chicago Press, 1975), p. 103.

15. Valdés, *La Escuela de Chicago*, p. 37.

16. Valdes, *La Escuela de Chicago*, p. 77.

17. Campero, *Los gremios empresariales*, p. 130.

18. Orlando Sáenz, "El Camino de Chile," January 9, 1974, cited in Campero, *Los gremios empresariales*, p. 105. The target of the last remark was obviously General Pinochet.

19. Ibid.

20. Campero arrives at a similar conclusion based on an analysis of the many statements by the business leadership between 1973 and 1975: "The handing over of economic policy occurred as a political option in the face of the crisis of 1974–75. The disagreements between the *gremios* and the government's technocratic team were stifled due to a fear of the political destabilization which disputes over economic policy might produce." And he adds the following revealing quotation from an interview granted to him by the ex-president of the National Industrial Society, Orlando Sáenz. "In

1973, the business sector did not have a national project.... If they had, they would not have let the Chicago Boys get their foot in the door. They would have defended their own political project.... In other words, it would have been this sector which replaced the political parties that had been withdrawn from circulation.... In the long run, the so-called national project of the Chicago Boys was more powerful than that which the business sector might have had." (Campero, *Los gremios impresariales*, p. 132)

21. Ricardo Lagos, "La Nouvelle Bourgeoisie," *Amerique Latine,* no. 6, CETRAL, Paris, 1981.

22. Ibid., p. 46.

23. Ibid., p. 47.

24. From a speech by General Leigh reproduced in *La Tercera,* January 11, 1975, quoted in Guillermo Campero and José Antonio Valenzuela, *El movimiento sindical en el régimen militar chileno* (Santiago: Instituto Latinoamericano de Estudios Transnacionales, 1984), p. 205.

25. Ibid., p. 208.

26. The sacking of General Leigh came about, as was shown in chapter 1, because of his opposition to the "national consultation" of 1978, which was supposed to support Pinochet in the face of "the international aggression against our country" and "reaffirm the legitimacy of the Government of the Republic as the sovereign body in the process of institutionalization." Both aspects were directly related to the internal competition that Leigh represented for the leadership. The international condemnation that most worried the government was the threat of a boycott from the AFL-CIO against Chilean exports because of the regime's refusal to cede any legal space to Chilean unions. The importance accorded to the process of institutionalization also clearly reflected the pressure of the air force to create a corporatist labor regime that would counterbalance the growing power of the financial-economic groups.

27. *Qué Pasa,* December 27, 1979, quoted in Valdés, *La Escuela de Chicago,* p. 32.

28. Eugenio Tironi, *Autoritarismo, modernización y marginalidad* (Santiago: Ediciones SUR, 1990). For a detailed study of this reform, see José Pablo Arellano, *Politicas sociales y desarollo: Chile, 1924–1984* (Santiago: CIEPLAN, 1986).

29. José Pablo Arellano, "Sistemas alternativos de Seguridad Social: Un análasis de la experiencia chilena" (Santiago: CIEPLAN, 1980).

30. A basic formulation of this philosophy can be found in ODEPLAN, *Informe Social, 1983* (Santiago, 1984). The immediate effects of the targeting policies, however, often included a growing segregation of the poor population and a fall in the quality of the assistance they received. A summary of conclusions reached in 1986 in various areas of social policy can be found in Javier Martínez, *Efectos sociales de la crisis económica: Chile, 1980–1985* (Santiago: CEPAL, Social Development Department, 1986).

31. Jarpa was the prototype of the traditional Chilean landowner. He had been the undisputed leader of opposition to Salvador Allende and, without doubt, a decisive factor in the growing radicalization of the anti-Allende movement (which included the Christian Democrats). His relations with

the *gremio* movement, and particularly with the small and medium business sectors, remained intact and he was thus a symbol of the unity of all the *gremios* with respect to the original military intervention. Jarpa had a long corporatist history. In contrast to many right-wing leaders whose origins lay in democratic organizations, whether conservative or liberal, Jarpa had come out of one of the many nationalist authoritarian groups that had supported the populist leadership of General Carlos Ibáñez del Campo in the first half of the 1950s.

32. Campero, *Los gremios empresariales*, p. 305.

33. For a detailed analysis of these measures, see chapter 2.

## Chapter 4

1. Since 1986 the following definition of employed and unemployed persons has been utilized by the National Statistical Institute of Chile in its labor force surveys:

(a) an employed person is anyone who during the week preceding the interview ( 1 ) engaged in one or more hours of remunerated work in the employ of others (whether waged or salaried, on commission or remunerated in kind); or as an employer or self-employed person (such as farmers, merchants, independent workers, or other professionals); or in unremunerated family labor involving an average of at least fifteen hours of work per week; or ( 2 ) despite having a job or owning a business, did not work during that week due to vacations, short-term illness, permission to be temporarily absent, or for some other reason.

(b) an unemployed person is anyone who was not working during the week preceding the survey, and ( 1 ) had previous regular work experience, and desired and had actively sought work at some point during the preceding two months, but had not been able to find it; or ( 2 ) had no previous regular employment but wanted to work for the first time and had attempted during the previous two months to obtain employment.

2. The term "wage relation" comes from regulation theory. See Robert Boyer, *Teoría de la regulación* (Sao Paulo: Editorial Brasiliense, 1988).

3. Eugenio Tironi and Javier Martínez, "Clase obrera y modelo económico: Un estudio del peso y la estructura del proletariado en Chile, 1960–1980," Working Paper 15 (Santiago: SUR, 1983).

4. Waged work is defined here as the sum of all workers and salaried employees counted in the quarterly employment surveys of the National Statistical Institute of Chile (INE). Persons in military service or associated with emergency work programs are not included in the category of waged work.

5. The rate of waged work is understood as the waged work force, defined in note 4, divided by the total work force of the country. It is difficult to compare the rate of waged work during the 1990s with the period before 1973, since the censuses of 1960 and 1970 tended to overestimate the situation in the countryside by considering all *inquilinos* (tenants enjoying usufruct of a plot of land in return for a contribution of family labor to the landlord) as waged workers. A significant proportion of all *inquilinos* re-

ceived up to 50 percent of their incomes in nonwage forms before the 1970s. At the same time, the employment surveys of the National Statistical Institute after 1976 have tended to underestimate agricultural wage labor by considering seasonal pieceworkers to be self-employed.

6. It would seem that in 1960 there were more than twice the number of waged workers per employer as in 1990. This must be taken, however, as only a rough approximation, since information from the 1970 census is being compared with the annual average figure provided by the national employment survey of INE. The first source shows fifty workers per employer in 1960, and the second suggests eighteeen workers per employer for 1990.

7. Víctor Tokman, "Tecnología para el sector informal urbano," Occasional Document 19 (Santiago: PREALC, 1978).

8. Javier Martínez and Arturo León, *Clases y clasificaciones sociales: Investigaciones sobre la estructura social chilena, 1970–1983* (Santiago: CED-SUR, 1987).

9. Joseph Ramos, "Segmentación del mercado de capital y empleo," *Trimestre Económico*, vol. 202 (April–June 1984); and *Urbanización y sector informal en América Latina* (Santiago: PREALC, 1991).

10. Norberto García and Víctor Tokman, "Transformación ocupacional y crisis," *Revista de la Cepal*, no. 24 (1984).

11. Aníbal Pinto, "Metropolización y terciarización: Malformaciones estructurales en el desarrollo latinoamericano," *Revista de la Cepal*, no. 24 (1984).

12. PREALC also excludes all those who work in the agricultural, fishing, and mining sectors.

13. Jaime Gatica, "La evolución del empleo formal e informal en el sector servicios latinoamericano," Document 279 (Santiago: PREALC, 1986).

14. See Alvaro Díaz, "La reestructuración industrial autoritaria en Chile," *Revista Proposiciones,* no. 17 (1989).

15. Alejandro Portes, Manuel Castells, and Lauren Benton, *The Informal Economy: Studies in Advanced and Less Developed Countries* (Johns Hopkins University Press, 1989), p. 11.

16. Tironi and Martínez, "Clase obrera y modelo económico," p. 201.

17. Gilbert Mathias and Pierre Salama, *O estado superdesenvolvido das metrópoles ao Terceiro Mundo* (São Paulo: Editorial Brasiliense, 1986); and Vicente Espinoza, "Networks of Informal Economy: Work and Community among Santiago's Poor," Ph.D. thesis, University of Toronto, 1992.

18. Díaz, "La reestructuración industrial autoritaria en Chile."

19. This point is made by Hernando de Soto, *El otro sendero* (Lima: Ed. Oveja Negra, 1986).

20. Analysis of 1960–85 is based on estimates from Esteban Jádresic, *Evolución del empleo y desempleo en Chile, 1970–1985: Series anuales y trimestrales*, Colección Estudios CIEPLAN, no. 20 (1986).

21. Ramos, "Segmentación del mercado de capital y empleo"; and Pinto, "Metropolización y terciarización." These arguments were published in the *CEPAL Review* in December 1984. A critical résumé of the debate, as well as discussion of the empirical evidence, can be found in Gatica, "La evolución del empleo formal e informal."

22. Gatica, "La evolución del empleo formal e informal."

23. These figures show tertiary employment with respect to total employment, not the economically active labor force, since unemployment would have distorted the analysis.

24. Gatica, "La evolución del empleo formal e infomal." This is not meant to suggest that services are unproductive.

25. Ramos, "Segmentación del mercado de capital y empleo."

26. Pinto, "Metropolización y terciarización."

27. Government of Chile, Ministerio de Planificación y Cooperación, *Encuesta de Caracterización Socioeconómica Nacional*, 1990 survey.

28. The growth of the average wage in relation to the minimum wage in fact illustrates increasing differentiation in the wage structure of Chile.

29. Studies carried out by PREALC, CEPAL, SUR, PET, CED, and CIEPLAN, Santiago de Chile

30. See Alejandro Mardónez Martínez and Pablo Sierra, *Los servicios al productor: Un análisis para el caso del cobre en Chile,* CEPAL, March 1991.

31. Between 1980 and 1990, employment in the transport sector grew by 47 percent, while the number of transport employers quadrupled.

32. Francisco León, "El empleo temporal en la agricultura chilena, 1976–1990," CELADE-OPS, Santiago, 1991.

33. Celia Montero, "La industria de la construcción en Chile y Argentina," prepared for CNRS-ORSTOM, Paris, 1988.

34. León, "El empleo temporal en la agricultura chilena."

## Chapter 5

1. Translator's note: The reference is to a pro-Pinochet account, Joaquín Lavín, *La revolución silenciosa* (Santiago: Editorial ZigZag, 1987).

# Index